What Does Not Change

What Does Not Change

The Significance of Charles Olson's "The Kingfishers"

Ralph Maud

Madison • Teaneck
Fairleigh Dickinson University Press
London: Associated University Presses

© 1998 by Associated University Presses, Inc.

All rights reserved. Authorization to photocopy items for internal or personal use, or the internal or personal use of specific clients, is granted by the copyright owner, provided that a base fee of $10.00, plus eight cents per page, per copy is paid directly to the Copyright Clearance Center, 222 Rosewood Drive, Danvers, Massachusetts 01923. [0-8386-3731-0/98 $10.00+8¢ pp, pc.]

Associated University Presses
440 Forsgate Drive
Cranbury, NJ 08512

Associated University Presses
16 Barter Street
London WC1A 2AH, England

Associated University Presses
P.O. Box 338, Port Credit
Mississauga, Ontario
Canada L5G 4L8

The paper used in this publication meets the requirements of the American National Standard for Permanence of Paper for Printed Library Materials Z39.48–1984.

Library of Congress Cataloging-in-Publication Data

Maud, Ralph.
    What does not change : the significance of Charles Olson's "The Kingfishers" / Ralph Maud.
      p.   cm.
    Includes bibliographical references and index.
    ISBN 0-8386-3731-0 (alk. paper)
    1. Olson, Charles, 1910–1970. Kingfishers. 2. Postmodernism (Literature)—United States. I. Title.
PS3529.L655K536 1998
811'.54—dc21   97-14291
                                                                           CIP

PRINTED IN THE UNITED STATES OF AMERICA

Contents

Bibliographic Abbreviations   7

Introduction   13
1. Anti-Wasteland   21
2. Politics   33
3. Modes of Form   44
4. Recurrences   61
5. Self   73
6. Pejorocracy   85
7. The Advantage   94
8. "The Praises"   108
9. "The Kingfishers": Epilogue   122

Appendices   132
Notes   160
Index   170

Bibliographic Abbreviations

Additional Prose = Charles Olson, *Additional Prose*, ed. George F. Butterick (Bolinas: Four Seasons Foundation, 1974).

boundary 2 = Matthew Corrigan, ed., "Charles Olson: Essays, Reminiscences, Reviews," *boundary 2*, vol. 2, nos. 1 and 2 (fall 1973/winter 1974).

Butterick = George Butterick, "Charles Olson's 'The Kingfishers' and the Poetics of Change," *American Poetry* 6:2 (winter 1989): 28–69.

Call Me Ishmael = Charles Olson, *Call Me Ishmael* (New York: Reynal and Hitchcock, 1947; reprint, San Francisco: City Lights Books, 1958).

Charles Olson's Reading = Ralph Maud, *Charles Olson's Reading* (Carbondale: Southern Illinois University Press, 1996).

Clark = Tom Clark, *Charles Olson: The Allegory of a Poet's Life* (New York: Norton, 1991).

Collected Poems = Charles Olson, *The Collected Poems of Charles Olson*, ed. George F. Butterick (Berkeley: University of California Press, 1987).

Corman Correspondence = Charles Olson and Cid Corman, *Complete Correspondence 1950–1964*, ed. George Evans, 2 vols (Orono: National Poetry Foundation, University of Maine, 1987 and 1991).

Creeley Correspondence = Charles Olson and Robert Creeley, *The Complete Correspondence*, vols 1–8, ed. George F. Butterick, vols 9 and 10, ed. Richard Blevins (Santa Rosa: Black Sparrow Press, 1980–96).

Dahlberg Correspondence = Paul Christensen, ed., *In Love, In Sorrow: The Complete Correspondence of Charles Olson and Edward Dahlberg* (New York: Paragon House, 1990).

Davenport = Guy Davenport, "Scholia and Conjectures for Olson's 'The Kingfishers,'" *boundary 2*: 250–68; collected in his *Geogra-*

phy of the Imagination (San Francisco: North Point Press, 1981).

Duberman = Martin Duberman, *Black Mountain: An Exploration in Community* (New York: Dutton, 1972); the Anchor Books 1973 reprint has different pagination.

Fiery Hunt = Charles Olson, *The Fiery Hunt and Other Plays* (Bolinas: Four Seasons Foundation, 1977).

Ghyka = Matila Ghyka, *The Geometry of Art and Life* (New York: Sheed and Ward, 1946).

Guide = George F. Butterick, *A Guide to the Maximus Poems of Charles Olson* (Berkeley: University of California Press, 1978).

Harris = Mary Emma Harris, *The Arts at Black Mountain College* (Cambridge: MIT Press, 1987).

Human Universe = Charles Olson, *Human Universe and Other Essays*, ed. Donald Allen (New York: Grove Press, 1967).

Maximus Poems = Charles Olson, *The Maximus Poems*, ed. George F. Butterick (Berkeley: University of California Press, 1983).

Minutes = *Minutes of the Charles Olson Society*, ed. Ralph Maud 1 (January 1993)–18 (November 1996).

Muthologos = Charles Olson, *Muthologos: The Collected Lectures and Interviews*, vols. 1 and 2, ed. George F. Butterick (Bolinas: Four Seasons Foundation, 1978).

Nation of Nothing But Poetry = Charles Olson, *A Nation of Nothing but Poetry: Supplementary Poems*, ed. George F. Butterick (Santa Rosa: Black Sparrow Press, 1989).

OLSON = *OLSON: The Journal of the Charles Olson Archive*, ed. George Butterick, 1 (spring 1974)–10 (fall 1978).

Olson/Melville = Ann Charters, *Olson/Melville: A Study in Affinity* (Berkeley: Oyez, 1968).

Payne Correspondence = "Montevallo and Montenegro: The Correspondence of Robert Payne and Charles Olson," *Minutes* 14 (April 1996).

Plutarch = C. W. King, trans., *Plutarch's Morals, Theosophical Essays* (London: George Bell, 1882).

Post Office = Charles Olson, *The Post Office: A Memoir of His Father* (Bolinas: Grey Fox Press, 1975).

Prescott = William H. Prescott, *History of the Conquest of Mexico and History of the Conquest of Peru* (New York: Modern Library, n.d.).

Seelye = Catherine Seelye, ed., *Charles Olson and Ezra Pound: An Encounter at St. Elizabeths* (New York: Grossman Publishers, 1975).

Selected Writings = *Selected Writings of Charles Olson*, ed. Robert Creeley (New York: New Directions, 1966).

Special View of History = Charles Olson, *The Special View of History*, ed. Ann Charters (Berkeley: Oyez, 1970).

Storrs = The Charles Olson Archive, Thomas J. Dodd Research Center, University of Connecticut, Storrs.

Von Hallberg = Robert von Hallberg, *Charles Olson: The Scholar's Art* (Cambridge: Harvard University Press, 1978).

What Does Not Change

Introduction

I

In trying to define "postmodern," Sherman Paul reckoned that its "advent may be marked by the publication in 1950 of Olson's 'Projective Verse,' an essay comparable in importance to Pound's early essays and notes on poetry."[1] Edward Halsey Foster noted that "Projective Verse" was "quickly recognized as a major statement for avant-garde poetics. William Carlos Williams excerpted sections of it in his autobiography, and it was crucial in defining the directions followed by poets as otherwise diverse as Allen Ginsberg, Michael McClure, and Jeremy Prynne."[2] Foster also perceived that Olson's "Projective Verse" essay was largely an exposition of "what he had done in 'The Kingfishers.'" The celebrity of the "influential essay"[3] is all the more reason to go behind it to the poetic praxis without which it would not have been written.

The present volume rises to the challenge of examining closely "The Kingfishers" (and the similarly pertinent, though not so well-known poem "The Praises") in order that the poetry that brought into existence "Projective Verse" might become a graspable artifact.

Focusing on the years 1948–49 holds out the pleasure of experiencing Charles Olson coming into his own as a poet. This is not only before "Projective Verse," but before the correspondence with Robert Creeley, before the first *Maximus* poem, before the trip to Yucatan, and before full-time residence at Black Mountain College. It is a time when Olson as a poet was quite unknown—for the simplest of reasons: he had only just embarked on the path of the poet, in January 1945, to be precise, when he was thirty-five years old. Like anyone else, he had written love poems in his younger days. These are found at the beginning of the magisterial *Collected Poems* edited by George Butterick for the University of California Press in 1987. "The Kingfishers" is on p. 86 of that six hundred-page volume and would be counted as juvenilia if Olson had not come to poetry as a grown man, a man whose genius had exhibited itself in two careers already, a man of the world in several senses: which meant that even his early poems were poems of experience.

Olson's innocence had been nurtured through his college years by Emerson's ideal of the American Scholar; he lost it by following Herman Melville into the tragic depths of *Moby-Dick*. In 1932 Olson completed a brilliant B.A. at Wesleyan University, Connecticut, and continued there to run through Melville's whole life and works for his M.A. And then it hit him. He was detective enough to track down many of Melville's own books; so one day he was looking at Melville's marginal notes in the Shakespeare volumes where Edmund in *King Lear* denies he is a traitor and says he will prove his honor, and there he found Melville's footnote: "The infernal nature has a valor often denied to innocence."[4] Olson realized what Melville meant by saying he had written "a wicked book." Ahab had been given a valor that the "right reason" of Starbuck and others did not have. Out of this understanding Olson wrote an essay, "Lear and Moby-Dick, " which was taken up by Dorothy Norman for the first issue of her prestigious *Twice A Year* (fall-winter 1938). Olson was twenty-eight years old.

By that time, after borrowing Olson's Melville discoveries for use in his forthcoming *American Renaissance*,[5] F. O. Matthiessen had already brought him into the graduate program at Harvard University and was now sponsoring him for a Guggenheim Fellowship. Olson got the Guggenheim, and studied and wrote for a year, mainly in Gloucester in cold and isolation. He was reenacting the dreadful self-exactitude of Melville's Pierre. He wrote with intensity and insight—there are many piles of his manuscripts in the Olson Archive at the University of Connecticut, Storrs. But the work stayed in manuscript. Olson never submitted it for a Ph.D. and he was saved from the vortex only by the love of the woman who became his wife and by the friend—the strange and talented Italian artist, Corrado Cagli—who, for Olson, was Senor Bagatto of the Tarot, the master magician. The first thing Olson did after the war was complete his Melville work as a book totally different from the dissertation he had written and overwritten. This was the lean and provocative *Call Me Ishmael* (published in March

1947), which caused a sensation in the academic world. But by then Olson had found a new pathway. He was a poet.

The highest of academic success had been in Olson's grasp, but a fatality in his nature spared him. A similar thing happened in his second career. What Olson did during the war as associate chief of the Foreign Language Division of the Office of War Information from 1942 to 1944 placed him strategically in Washington for a successful career in politics. Olson's role in the 1944 reelection of Franklin D. Roosevelt and the probability of a government appointment in January 1945—all this takes us so directly into the making of "The Kingfishers" that we will be looking at it in some detail later. But because we are talking about the author of a modern epic, *The Maximus Poems*, and not about a Secretary of State or Commerce, needless to say, Olson's inner stem of stubbornness saved him again. Olson as an Ivy League Professor of American Literature or Olson as a United States cabinet veteran, either of these lives would have been interesting to follow; but we have it better yet when these two lives are absorbed into that of a poet ambitious to prove that as a poet he is no less a man than he would have been in either of those previous worlds.

II

Can we get some sense of the man at the time he wrote "The Kingfishers"? In 1940 he had met Constance Wilcock, and they had lived together first in New York and since September 1942 in Washington, D.C. Connie worked at various secretarial and administrative jobs, so that Olson was able to spend his days (that is, usually working nights and sleeping days) in the inner-city retreat they had discovered at 217 Randolph Place NE. Olson gives a charming thumbnail sketch in a letter to Creeley of 30 May 1950 (*Creeley Correspondence*, 1:59): "have come in from sittin with constanza lookin at the jungle of our garden, the hidden garden which lured us to live here, hidden, that is, as right rapture in this Dead City, like a rose among the broken bottles of the freight yd behind." He relishes the isolation of "this small two room jewel in brick" (*Creeley Correspondence*, 1:136). Frank Moore has drawn a plan of the small house from memory in *Minutes of the Charles Olson Society* 11 (November 1995). He often slept as a visitor in the entrance way to the other room, which was living room, dining room, library, as well as the Olsons' bedroom. Moore tells us that when Olson sat at the table with his back to the fireplace he could not stretch his legs without coming up against the bed with his feet. The shower was in the basement down a staircase that made Fielding Dawson stoop when he stayed there.[6] The place gave a "heightened sense of Olson's bulk," according to Elizabeth von Thurn, who came there with Frank Moore. It "simply wasn't big enough to contain him, his gestures and his words, but somehow the setting was exactly right: seclusion, but wall and voids to wrestle with."[7] (We might remember this description when we later hear Olson talking about "containment" as a most important corrective to free verse.) Into this Randolph Place world there are some welcome intrusions: "the birds, bugs, cats, dogs like it—shit, screw, nest, sing; and the Negroes, who used to drink muscatel down on the tracks (B & O) a block away, now come in, that the gate's gone, and have themselves a time, under the patched french windows 10 feet over their head, where we sleep" (*Creeley Correspondence*, 1:136). There were also the unwelcome intrusions of the landlady. But all in all it proved to be a good place to get work done.

"I never felt days and weeks slip away as these," Olson wrote to his friend Monroe Engel on 6 April 1949. "I have been trying myself out on a long poem. . . . I have no idea what it is or if it has value. But the way it has unfolded, so much as my mind contains of it, it is a long job."[8] When he adds, "I have not isolated myself to it," he is not referring to physical isolation (which was, as we have seen, an enabling factor) but to other intellectual work that went on alongside the writing of "The Kingfishers," chiefly an essay on Melville and Homer, utilizing his new discovery, Victor Bérard's extensive research on the *Odyssey* in French, with the sole English translation *Did Homer Live?* (New York: Dutton 1931). There may be some relaxation for us in knowing, as we enter an explication of "The Kingfishers," that it does not contain absolutely everything that Olson was interested in. The poem was not a gall stone demanding all his attention in its passing.

There were also the visits to Black Mountain College: the first, 12–16 October 1948; the second, 17–21 November 1948; the third, 14–21 December 1948; and the fourth—which would be during the actual writing of "The Kingfishers"—14–20 February 1949. "Black

Mountain has helped," Olson wrote Engel in the letter cited, "for I am able to lecture on those things which concern me at the time, and there is no break in stride. Yet it brings change." Taking on these week-long visits is part of Olson's own "will to change." As he wrote to Robert Payne in a letter just after the first visit: "something very essential happened on that sidehill in North Carolina, some touch with a source of force."[9]

Black Mountain was the source of some specific details of "The Kingfishers," as we shall see, but it was not where the writing got done. It was too much like giving a pint of blood each day for a week. Washington—217 Randolph Place anyway—was the workplace. "The present year has been a sort of a fruitage of this place and this life," Olson wrote Engel from Washington in the 6 April 1949 letter. "I have stayed reasonably content and organized.... So here I am, stuck, or charmed." This, then, is the context for the writing of "The Kingfishers." Olson was stuck with it as a self-imposed task; and, when he found it falling through repeated attention into proper form, he was charmed, gratified by the rhythms the ideas of the poem generated. So that when he was sending it off for publication he could refer to it as the poem "which i value more than anything i have written."[10]

III

Donald Allen's anthology *The New American Poetry: 1945–1960*, published by Grove Press in the first year of the decade, was carried around in many backpacks during the 1960s and has become a milestone in literary history.[11] Charles Olson was first up to bat in *The New American Poetry*, and so it turned out that the first poem in the anthology was "The Kingfishers." It is a poem, then, that has had its share of attention. Many on the road must have felt some confirmation for their lifestyle in the opening assertion of the poem:

What does not change / is the will to change.

And Fernand—

> he who said, "The kingfishers!
> who cares
> for their feathers
> now?"

—Fernand became a sort of talisman, a mysterious figure that reverberated with many possibilities. And the last line of the poem,

> I hunt among stones

gave a sense of a preparatory state that many may have felt was their own condition. "The Kingfishers" was taken as a poem, perhaps *the* poem, of its time. Because we have not yet digested fully either the time or the poem, that work still stands before us to do.

This *explication du texte* of "The Kingfishers" is long overdue. In the late 1960s, my friend Guy Davenport, preparing to teach "The Kingfishers" in class, began asking around and discovered that "none of the admirers of the poem had the least notion as to the meaning of any of the allusions, obscure or otherwise."[12] In particular, as he noted in the extensive explication he published in the Olson memorial volume of *boundary 2* in 1974, "Fernand is a mystery: a survey of Olson's circle and scholars has failed to turn up any identification at all."[13] When I came to teach "The Kingfishers" myself, I too was exasperated. I found Davenport's piece useful, but continually provocative in its errancies. I felt I had to be able to do better—or at least that must have been the impression I gave when I dropped in to see Guy in Lexington in 1978. He took me at what must have been my word; and in his Arthur and Margaret Glasgow Lecture at Washington and Lee University in 1985, as a postscript to describing his own adventures with "The Kingfishers," he said: "I have discovered since that Ralph Maud, at Simon Fraser University, was working parallel to my research; he still is. His study, when it is published, will be better than mine."[14] I became aware of this generous testimonial seven years ago, and it made me very uncomfortable because I still did not know who Fernand was!

All who work in the field of Olson scholarship are indebted to the late George Butterick, the founder (with Charles Boer) of the Olson Archive at Storrs and its first accomplished curator. George, as a matter of fact, knew for quite a while who Fernand was. But only in an article in *American Poetry* (Winter 1989), published just before his untimely death, did he find the proper format for revealing Fernand's identity in all its ordinariness.[15] With that revelation Butterick pressed the release-catch for the full-scale explication of "The Kingfishers" that I had in mind.

I have a great indebtedness to previous commentators, especially George Butterick. Where my indebtedness is specific and palpable, I have acknowledged it at the appropriate place in the body of this book. The broader debt, which I should speak of here, is that of not having had to be the first to try to fathom this difficult (or so it must seem at first glance) poem. It makes for a certain assurance to know what difficulties have remained after others have had their say and that one is, therefore, filling genuine gaps in knowledge.

I have benefited very much in this proceeding by having had Charles Watts, Sharon Thesen, and Robin Blaser as interested consultants locally, and the late John Clarke as correspondent. I am happy that *intent.* magazine printed some of my early stabs at explication in issue nos. 2 and 3. I am indebted to George Bowering for putting me on to the Italian version of George Butterick's 1989 article, and to Clayton Eshleman for a similar service regarding the *American Poetry* printing of it.

I would like to acknowledge with thanks the libraries holding manuscript material used in this volume: Harry Ransom Humanities Research Center, University of Texas, Austin; Lilly Library, Indiana University; University of Kansas Library, Lawrence; Special Collections Library, Stanford; Lockwood Library of the State University of New York, Buffalo; Special Collections Library, State University of New York at Stony Brook; Beinecke Library, Yale University; Special Collections Library, University of Southern Illinois, Carbondale; Houghton Library, Harvard University; Archives of American Art, New York City; Contemporary Literature Collection, Simon Fraser University, Burnaby, B.C.; Special Collections Library, Wesleyan University, Middletown; State Archives of North Carolina, Raleigh; and chiefly the Olson Archive in the Special Collections Library of the University of Connecticut,

Storrs, where the help of Richard Schimmelpfeng and Richard Fyffe has been most facilitating. James Laughlin opened his own library to me with great generosity.

This book is dedicated to Harry Keyishian because, among other things, he (literally) introduced Charles Olson to me.

Previously unpublished writings by Charles Olson are printed through the courtesy of the Archives and Special Collections Department, Thomas J. Dodd Research Center, University of Connecticut Library. Copyright © 1996 by the University of Connecticut Library, Storrs. All rights reserved.

1
Anti-Wasteland

I

At one of the stages on the road to "The Kingfishers," Olson wrote to his friend Robert Payne: "I had locked myself in for three weeks in an attempt to do a 1st long poem. Yesterday I put it together and looked it over, compared it to THE WASTELAND, and decided, as a practicer of the gentle craft, I better do more work at the last."[1] It is not surprising that a new poet in 1949, setting out to write a poem of importance to his own time, would feel he had to assess it against T. S. Eliot's "The Waste Land," long taken to be the most accurate image of the age.

Sitting with Dorothy Pound and St.-John Perse, Olson was in the audience when Eliot read at the National Gallery in Washington in May 1947. The visitor struck the resident Washingtonian as the ultimate in a series of "'Poets'" making a pilgrimage "as tho to Rome" for a "laying on of hands." It was, he feared, "the coming into existence of an american poet laureate."[2] Olson instinctively allied himself with the stay-at-home American writers, led by William Carlos Williams, who had always had reservations about Eliot. Williams's scathing attack in *Four Pages* (February 1948) began: "That Mr. T. S. Eliot is an idiot I see no reason to insist. No one who has wheedled himself into the good graces of the Church of England, in fact the British Empire, Harvard University (an honorary LLD) and the Nobel Prize Committee can be considered that."[3] After reading this satirical article on Eliot's reversing himself on Milton, Olson wrote to Williams: "you have roused us all with the magnificent trip-up of Eliot. You sure took his pants down" (unpublished letter of 24 February 1948 at Yale). Olson presumably took particular note of Williams's opinion there that Eliot was now as much a "barrier to the young" as

Milton had been: "He is already the 'old' . . . something for the young to escape also if they are to get forward with a style and a vigor of style which calls them today." Olson was thirty-eight at this time, but having been a declared poet for precisely three years he might have felt the applicability to himself of that word "young."

Olson had his own unique grudge against Eliot. "I have never forgiven Eliot," he wrote in his March 1949 letter to Payne, "for stealing Dry Salvages from me." This is the reiteration of a complaint he made in a session with Ezra Pound at St. Elizabeths on 19 March 1946 (Seelye, p. 78). It is the budding Gloucester poet's annoyance that Eliot had got in there before him, using the three local islands called "The Dry Salvages" for one of his *Four Quartets*. When Olson on a trip to Gloucester on 14 June 1947 sent Pound a picture postcard of the statue of the Lady of Good Voyage on top of the Portuguese Church and penned the message, "Here is my Lady that Possum stole,"[4] he had in mind a passage from part IV of Eliot's poem:

> Lady, whose shrine stands on the promontory,
> Pray for all those who are in ships, those
> Whose business has to do with fish, and
> Those concerned with every lawful traffic

—beautiful lines, as everyone including Olson would agree.[5] However, in this poem purporting to be about Cape Ann, is there anything, Olson would want to ask, of the real Gloucester? Does Eliot know what having to do with fish really involves, in economic and human terms? In invoking the "Lady" so vaguely, does he not know that the statue is not on a promontory but on a church-top in the middle of the town? Does he not know that she has in her arms no infant Saviour but a fishing schooner? Olson's point of contention is particularity. It can be confirmed from the record what Olson only guessed at: that Eliot had not been back to Gloucester since 1915, that he did not, in fact, remember a Lady of Good Voyage, but only thought "that there *ought* to be a shrine of the B.V.M. at the harbour mouth of a fishing port."[6] Helen Gardner reveals that Eliot was actually thinking of the Church of Notre Dame de la Gard high over the sea at Marseilles and others like that. In 1961 Eliot wrote to a Rev. W. T. Levy who had commented on this passage in "The Dry Salvages": "You accepted it as a class of churches, and were not thinking of a particular church. And that is the right way to think of it. It is fortuitous in our case that I as a writer and you as reader of these lines happened to know and react identically."[7] Eliot has found a kin in the Rev. W. T. Levy. They share a generalizing mode. This is not surprising, because it is the operative frame most comfortable to Western thinking, the inherited attitude we are all familiar with from Greece, Rome, and the Royal Society. It is also exactly what Olson is up in arms against: "Particularism has to be fought for, anew."[8] Olson feels no kinship with the Rev. W. T. Levy. When he is content to think in terms of "a class of churches," the Rev. W. T. Levy does not know what Olson insists upon in his "Human Universe" essay:

> that a thing, any thing, impinges on us by a more important fact, its self-existence . . . the very character of it which calls our attention to it, which wants us to know more about it, its particularity. This is what we are confronted by, not the thing's "class."[9]

In complaining to Payne (in the letter cited previously) Olson referred to Eliot's use of the "longshore fisherman" in "The Waste Land" as well as that of the "Lady" in "The Dry Salvages": if these are "a measure of his use of other experience, then he lacks economic root. And he will turn out to be romantic." Even when Eliot seems so specific with his "pleasant whining of a mandolin . . . where fishermen lounge at noon," his pseudoparticularity, as in "mandolin" and "noon," is essentially a distancing of himself from the real condition of things: so Olson's argument would go. Eliot steals the Lady of Good Voyage by generalizing her, divorcing her from the economics of Gloucester. Consequently, there is only sentiment.

By 16 May 1950, when Olson is repeating the same complaint in a letter to Robert Creeley as "one particularist to another," he is ready to reconstitute his anger at Eliot's "use of my, *my* madonna, buono viaggi, Gloucester, and how he misuses it, is riding, is generalizer" (*Creeley Correspondence* 1, p. 28). He sits down that very day to start the first of the *Maximus Poems*, in the course of which he reclaims his Lady:

> o my lady of good voyage
> in whose arms, whose left arm rests
> no boy but a carefully carved wood, a painted face, a schooner?[10]

—also stressing the economic reality: "moneys are, facts! / facts, to be dealt with, as the sea is."

Meanwhile, in a preliminary way, in the early months of 1949, Olson was approaching a final form for "The Kingfishers" in a like mood of antagonism to the "generalizing humanism"[11] that Eliot was seen to stand for. It is impossible to underestimate the strategic importance of this poem in its adversarial role, leading up to the major question in the "Human Universe" essay: "Can one re-state man in any way to repossess him of his dynamic?"[12]—with its answer: because Western Civilization has brought us to ruin, to achieve some kind of solution one must go *back* before the Greek philosophers, and *out* into still living primitive societies. No one, not even D. H. Lawrence, had been so radically modern in challenging rationalism with recourse to its opposite. Olson, as we shall further note, had to coin the word "postmodern" for this push into the future from the vantage of the archaic past. The last line of "The Kingfishers"—"I hunt among stones"—has really none of the anomie of "The Waste Land" but, in keeping with the overall assertive tone of the poem, represents a state of readiness for a new active future. Referring to "The Kingfishers" in particular, the critic M. L. Rosenthal has said: "His attempt is to isolate and resurrect primal values that have been driven out of sight by the alienating force of European civilization."[13] Because he has taken on the chief contemporary poet of European civilization and because he wants to propose a radical new attitude to the past and future, Olson—if he achieves his intention at all—will have made a considerable mark, will, in the words of Eric Mottram, have written with "The Kingfishers" and its "calculated," "daring" statements about culture "a major poem of this century."[14]

II

Was there ever a room in which women came and went, talking of Michelangelo? Anyone with insight into Eliot's idiom does not ask, knowing his remarkable talent for having a semblance of specificity endure as a universal feeling. As we have said, this is not Olson's way. It is a different kind of particularism he is fighting for anew. Taking, for instance, the particular proper name "Fernand" of the first part of "The Kingfishers," one might infer that its use by Olson resembles T. S. Eliot's use of "J. Alfred Prufrock" in some way. Fernand's "sliding along the wall of the night, losing himself in some crack in the ruins" (lines 11–12) appears at first glance similar to Prufrock's possible exit: "to turn back and descend the stair." But, again, if there was no actual room, there can be no such stair. To ask if Prufrock really had a bald spot is impertinent. That's not what Eliot meant at all. If, on the other hand, we ask Olson if there was an actual room in which Fernand "talked lispingly of Albers and Angkor Vat" (line 8), his answer is a definite yes. Just as the evocative quality of "The Love Song" is enhanced by the indeterminacy of Prufrock, so does the specificity of Fernand provide a proper ingress to a very different poem.

George Butterick in conversation with the poet in Gloucester in June 1968 learned that Fernand "had been a mutual guest at a party given by friends in Washington."[15] Some years later Butterick pursued this lead to a likely party giver, the Washington artist Peter Blanc, and received in answer to his enquiry an informative letter:

Fernand in fact was a John Gernand who worked as a kind of associate curator at the Phillips Gallery in Washington and was a painter in his own right. He was a quiet, gentle, introverted and perhaps slightly effeminate man. I saw him quite often at the Phillips Gallery but rarely any place else. I don't remember what prompted me to invite him to the little party at which Olson got his inspiration because I rarely saw him socially but in any case I did and he came and to my surprise got quickly and thoroughly plastered. My studio was a small one on the second floor of an old building in St. Matthews Court right behind St. Matthew's Cathedral. An outside iron staircase ran up to a bright red door. As a result of his heavy drinking John Gernand had begun to droop when suddenly to everyone's surprise he sprang to his feet and began struggling towards the door mumbling to himself. Just before he reached the door he lurched around and cried out: "The blue—the blue of the kingfisher's feather!" and with that he ran out the door and clattered down the iron steps into the night. Charles witnessed this incident I know because we exchanged glances and made some casual remark about it.[16]

So "Fernand" is not a made-up first name, as we might have supposed, but, in fact, an actual last name, Gernand, slightly misremembered by Olson.

As Butterick tells it in his article, Peter Blanc could not remember anything about the birds of the opening lines, which set the stage for the Fernand incident:

> when he came in, he had gone around the rooms
> and got them back in their cages, the green one first,
> she with the bad leg, and then the blue.
>
> (lines 4–6)

But then, prompted by Butterick's query, Joan Blanc found the copy of the *Montevallo Review* containing the first printing of "The Kingfishers," which was inscribed by Olson: "For Peter and Joan, whose birds. . . . In admiration, Charles." Peter Blanc wrote immediately to Butterick:

> This reminded me that early in my relationship with my wife she had kept two parakeets in her apartment, a green one with a crippled leg and a blue one. We often let them out of the cage and allowed them to fly freely in the rooms. . . . I must conclude that he visited the apartment one day when the birds were out and helped return them to their cage.[17]

What Olson once called the "tale of the guy and the birds"[18] is thus confirmed to be a slice of the same actuality as the Fernand episode. The poem has it as a sequence of events, remembered in a waking hangover the following day. Perhaps they were two separate events, conflated. In any case, the puzzle dissolves. We can even pin down the probable date of the party: in a letter to Caresse Crosby of 10 October 1948, Olson mentions having been to "Peter Blanc's Friday night," that is, 8 October 1948 (unpublished letter at Southern Illinois University).

The chief outstanding problem, before we get to Gernand's kingfishers themselves, is how such a garret party earns a place at the beginning of a poem meant to be of important substance. Well, we know that epics are supposed to begin in medias res. "He woke, fully clothed, in his bed" (line 2) would certainly, not to be flippant, count as such. Olson once told me (in relation to certain early *Maximus* poems, but I think it applies here too) that it is like a guitarist in a supper club—before he gets to the song, he has a little friendly patter with the audience, telling something of how the song came to be written, where it came from. It was not long after "The Kingfishers" was finished that Olson sent out to various friends a short poem that said:[19]

> These days
> whatever you have to say, leave
> the roots on, let them
> dangle
>
> And the dirt
>
> > just to make clear
> > where they come from.

We can think of the first page of "The Kingfishers" as showing the roots dangling. No matter how intellectual the poem may get, we are here told that it had its origin in an actual experience, something that struck the poet.

There is a note at Storrs in which Olson refers to this opening passage of "The Kingfishers" as "the phenomenology of the birds."[20] In Olson's phenomenology it is the *thing* that motivates the *response*. We are reminded of the confirmation that Olson later received for his position from Maurice Merleau-Ponty's *Phenomenology of Perception*, published in translation in 1962. In paraphrasing Merleau-Ponty to an audience on 16 November 1963, Olson stated that "the narrative that gets started begins to be the story that will yield from the object a *raison* that causes us in the first place to give our attention to it."[21] In other words, the birds demanded the poem; they are not there because the poem's subject suggested their appropriateness. At this initial stage, therefore, the poem's explication remains entirely with the objects themselves, what was given, what presented itself.

Likewise, it is clear that the kingfishers were not thought up by the poet to symbolize something. They were there before the poem. Gernand's riveting questions at the party, as remembered by Olson, "The kingfishers! / who cares / for their feathers / now?"

(lines 12–15) and "The pool   the kingfishers' feathers were wealth   why / did the export stop?" (lines 21–22)—this casual stranger's insistences gave Olson the poem. This was the totally unlikely Muse that Olson was fated to listen to and, in the traditional way of the epic, name in the opening lines as an invocation.

John Gernand is not being quoted as an authority but in an unexpected way turns out to have been one. From a brilliant piece of detective work by George Butterick we have a good idea what he had been reading to make him go on about Angkor Vat and kingfishers' feathers. Osbert Sitwell's travel book *Escape With Me!*, published in New York in 1940, takes the reader to the temples of Angkor Vat in Cambodia and asks where the vast revenue needed for the artwork and the upkeep of the buildings came from:

> And the answer, which I have never hitherto seen stated outright in print, is one of the strangest and most romantic that can be imagined: from the *wings of kingfishers* . . . their flashing and iridescent feathers were shipped to Canton, where they were fashioned into those glittering blue and green tiaras, worn, until recent years, by every Chinese bride.[22]

Angkor Vat's many artificial pools provided the habitat for the birds who financed the national architectural treasure. "Why did the export stop?" Gernand might well ask that question, for Sitwell has no definite information on the point. Suffice it to say, this travel book source provides an entirely satisfactory explanation of the "Fernand" passage, and we can banish from our minds any locale other than Angkor Vat that may have been proposed for the kingfishers, Yucatan or whatever.

Whether or not Olson himself found Osbert Sitwell's book and from it put words into Fernand's mouth we do not know. Peter Blanc remembers only one phrase, about the feathers being blue. Olson was capable of amplifying on the given. It would be an unattractive rigidity if he was not. "Albers" (line 8) is an added word; it was not present in the first draft of the line. If Gernand had actually mentioned Albers in his mutterings, it would have been quite a coincidence. The day before the party (reckoning that 8 October 1948 is the right date), Olson had just written to Josef Albers, then Rector of Black Mountain College, accepting his invitation to go there for a week, his first visit.[23] So that, assuming it was, indeed, the poet who injected the name, we see that it was more than to emphasize the lisping alliteration. Albers was equally a given.

III

There is another odd word in this passage, the curious use of the word "ruins" in lines 11–12: "he was already sliding along the wall of the night, losing himself / in some crack of the ruins." The first draft of these lines at Storrs is helpful: "When I saw him, he was at the door, all inside his narrows, / starting to slide along the wall of the night, to lose himself in some crack of the ruins." A gloss on "narrows" is found in a prose note in "The Kingfishers" file at Storrs, where Olson wrote: "The constant danger is the narrows of the self, the natural narrows. Only the mind and the heart can keep a man free."[24] If Fernand's "narrows" are his fixation on the kingfishers' feathers, then the "ruins" he loses himself in will be Angkor Vat, mentally arrested in a time warp. Not to make too much of Fernand, but the figure introducing the theme of change and loss into the poem is himself a loser. We might go further and take his disintegration as Western man's condition as a whole. Because we know that Olson had T. S. Eliot "very much in mind,"[25] he was probably thinking of the famous line near the end of "The Waste Land": "These fragments I have shored against my ruins." As a judgement on contemporary life, "The Kingfishers" and "The Waste Land" share the same vision—only Olson would not accept that his poem was made up of fragments. It is, as we hope to prove, making a coherent moral statement in an expositional mode.

But would it not be possible to stick with the literal here? Gernand was going down the stairs of "an old building in St. Matthews Court," as Peter Blanc described it in the letter to Butterick. This was right behind St. Matthews Cathedral. If not in a total state of disrepair, the church might still be thought of, without too much of a flight of fancy, as providing a crack in its ruins for Fernand to lose himself in. We should always favor the literal with Olson, who was not enamored of metaphor. We have seen him, in the letter to Creeley quoted in the introduction call Washington, D.C., "this Dead City." If Olson felt he was living in the "ruins" that

America's capital had become, he would not have felt the word as metaphor but as truth.

Unfortunately, "ruins" is too enticing a word. It led Guy Davenport to place "The Kingfishers" within the traditional genre of "meditation on ruins."[26] In his article in *boundary 2* (p. 250), he mentions several works in the genre, including Shelley's "Ozymandias" and Melville's "Clarel." He suggests specifically that Olson was stimulated by Pablo Neruda's "Macchu Picchu." It is possible that Olson could have read a translation prior to "The Kingfishers." One was published in *Tiger's Eye* 5 (October 1948). But I concur with Butterick that "there is not the slightest evidence" that he did. "Olson's constant, renowned borrowing—especially in this poem—encourages just such an overall sense of him as a derivative poet," Butterick writes in his *American Poetry* article (p. 57). "Mere comparisons and general parallels are not enough, however; in almost every case of borrowing throughout his work, the particular evidence is clear, some stain is there confirmable by the usual standards of evidence. Neruda was not one of his influences." At the same time, we should not hesitate to acknowledge one of the simplicities of the poem: that the kingfishers, in certain juxtapositions, come to be symbolic of Western civilization in ruins. In this sense, Olson shares Neruda's vision of capitalist degradation. As a vigorous poem about history, however, "The Kingfishers" is not a mere "meditation" on our bleak prospects—nor does it reduce to the mind-set of a Marxist solution.

In the word "ruins," there may too be something of an echo of what Olson on one of his visits to St. Elizabeths had heard Pound murmuring: "Among the ruins, among the ruins, the finest memory in the Orient."[27] He had read *The Pisan Cantos* and knew the feeling Pound put into his own fragments: "a man on whom the sun has gone down . . . a lone ant from a broken ant-hill."[28] But when Pound adds "from the wreckage of Europe," Olson knows he is lamenting the fall of Fascism. He cannot follow him there, any more than he can follow Neruda or Eliot into their cracks in the ruins.

Pound was harder to shake off. When he felt like it, Olson would call Pound his "master";[29] however, he did not care for other people saying it. One of the first reviews to mention "The Kingfishers" typed it as "an imitation of the base he has chosen—the *Cantos*."[30] "These idiots cry, 'Pound,'" Olson protested to Creeley; "the superficial resemblances (if there are such . . .) are used to beat me with" (*Creeley Correspondence* 7, p. 244). He cites specifically "The Kingfishers," which, though "time and again I have heard, 'Pound,' feels so completely mine." Because the poem was begun soon after the break with Pound in February 1948, one might expect it to be anti-Pound as well as anti-Eliot. It is, insofar as both those poets are ensconced in the "Western Box, Gemisto, 1429 A.D., up."[31] Olson is claiming for himself a "sense of life as wider, more objective than it is allowed to be within the morality and the subjectivism of the West." Revealing his belief that this involves a leap beyond Pound, he continues in this note to himself: "If you trust yr vocal roundness as a consequence of yr Objectivism, you need not worry one day. In this roundness you outdo Pound, whatever his scholastic power."[32]

IV

The Pound/Olson relationship is complicated and deserves more attention later. Olson's "Anti-Wasteland" push is easier to identify and understand as motivating "The Kingfishers." When Olson came to write his *ars poetica* "Projective Verse" in 1950, Eliot alone was named as a "nonprojective" poet, "a proof of present danger."[33] The phrasing of the first draft of the essay (enclosed in a letter to Frances Boldereff 11 February 1950 at Storrs) reveals even more of an animus than the published version in its use of an Elizabethan lisp: "OMeliot is *not* projective, goeth by his personeth instead of by object and by passion."

Conclusive evidence for all this is found in one of the earliest worksheets in the "Kingfishers" file at Storrs, where the heading is such that it has provided us with the title for this chapter:

> *Anti-Wasteland*
> I objective records & vistas of the city
> II the morning
>   the birds
> III (the desert become city
> IV (the city gone jungle
>   I–III recur)
> V the going on—change again
>   the *Long March*.

Though this plan was not carried out consistently, we can see some of the seminal notions that forced "The Kingfishers" into being. The stagnation of the "wasteland," where the desert, city, and jungle are in recurring flux, is to be directly opposed by the "going on" of the Long March of the Chinese Communist Army. It appears there is going to be a King Fisher to counter Eliot's Fisher King, and it looks a lot like Mao Tse-tung.

The general intention is clear. The specific moment of inception may well have been the Eliot evening at the Library of Congress in May 1947. George Butterick in his article imagines Olson listening to "Burnt Norton," that "distinctly motionless poem," which includes the following lines in part IV:

>   After the kingfisher's wing
> Has answered light to light, and is silent, the light is still
> At the still point of the turning world.

This "twittering world, rocking back and forth, never gaining an inch of change," Butterick feels, "might have been enough to send the younger writer home with renewed determination."[34]

2
Politics

I

"The job of the poet," Olson wrote in a Storrs notebook ("Key West II," entry dated 2 March 1945), "is to be destructive, to get rid of the dead past." The theme of this manifesto inaugurating his life as a poet is the will to change. "Two attitudes have life in them today—destruction and prophecy. All the middle ground—peace, progress, creating the balance of forces, pragmatism—" (i.e., all that Olson had been living by as a politician, supposedly) "is dull and fruitless." Therefore, the poet must be radical, in the sense of "to root out"; the poet must also be vatic: "To have the prophecy in him to know what is stirring in the womb of the present, to show the very age and body of the time its form and pressure." This is Olson at midlife, determined to get out of the dark forest. "The Kingfishers" has its inception in the determination to live up to this resolve: to know what is vital and, in discarding the rest, make it prevail. He wants to bring over into poetry the best of what he was as a politician: "The job, given the obsession I am a writer, to be as decisive, careless, productive, and direct as I was as politician!"[1]

Who was the politician that the poet felt he must keep faith with and surpass? It was the young man who, in September 1942, applied for work at the Foreign Language Division of the Office of War Information, and was hired by Alan Cranston at seventy-five dollars a week, to join such people as Archibald MacLeish, Robert Sherwood, John Houseman, and Elmer Davis in fighting the war of words. His window looked out on the Library of Congress, with its columns and dome. The new agency's big, open office, as described by Tom Clark in the chapter "The Trick of Politics (1942–1944)" in his biography, *Charles Olson: The Allegory of a Poet's Life* (pp. 76–77), was as crowded, noisy and bustling with activity as the city room of a large urban newspaper. It was an electrifying setting for Olson's entry to the arena of high-stakes political action. For the next few years he was to be not just a spectator but a player there. For him government service would indeed be a whole new kind of life, active, committed, and outward.

Ultimately, the bureaucracy became too much for Olson, and he resigned in May 1944 just in time to join the fight for Roosevelt's fourth term. He was in the thick of things at the Democratic Party convention in Chicago but had to watch Truman beat out Henry Wallace for the vice-president slot. As director of the Foreign Nationalities Division of the Democratic National Committee, Olson's job was to see that the eastern seaboard immigrant vote went to Roosevelt; he appears to have accomplished this. A conspicuous thing he did was introduce Frank Sinatra on the stage of Madison Square Garden during the rally "Everybody for Roosevelt" 2 November 1944. Because of his contribution to the election victory, he would have been in line for a good political patronage job. But, as he vacationed with other Democratic apparatchiks in Key West, waiting for Inauguration Day, he knew he had to make a change.

Olson might very well have gone back up to Washington in January 1945 like the rest of them. Partly, we conjecture, he disliked the cynicism of the party hacks. But there was also a more positive influence, that of Ernest Hemingway. Pauline, Hemingway's former wife, was still living in their Key West house, full of the writer's memorabilia and books. She loaned Olson and Connie the guest house "in return for their keeping an eye on her two teenage sons when she was away from home."[2] Olson worked at the same desk as Hemingway himself had and felt the presence of his ghost. It was in this setting that Olson committed himself to the life of the writer. Of significance is the fact that Olson's very first publication had been a review article in his college literary journal on Hemingway's *Death in the Afternoon*, in which he exhibited a knowledge of all Hemingway's writing up to that time.[3] We do not hear much from Olson on Hemingway later, but we do not need to to realize what an influence would be there at that crucial moment in January 1945. Hemingway was a decisive, careless, productive, and direct man, who was also a successful writer. Olson could be too.

Ruminating on this later, in a letter to Frances Boldereff of 27 July 1950, Olson wrote:

> I was—and it bothered me considerably—extremely clear, swift and all-one-piece when I was a man of action. . . . I was all synapse, rhythm, bones-making-straight-gestures-&-decisions, sex. You will imagine . . . how hard it was for me, in Key West, to put it aside, and take up this other struggle!

Four years after Key West, "The Kingfishers" is the first ambitious result of the decision. Still in the coils of the change, he was documenting it in the poem as decisively, as carelessly, as productively, and as directly as he knew how.

II

The theme is the will to change. Olson had demonstrated it in the telegram of resignation from Democratic Party politics, which became the poem "The K." It begins: "Take, then, my answer."[4] We are spectators of Olson's moment of choice. "The substance of life is change," he had written in an early notebook entry. "I expect and accept change."[5] But if one wants to change the world by changing oneself, it will take more than a telegram. That is only the beginning of a process of realignment, self-examination, and reformulation of the methodology for individual action in society. Olson put it nicely later, in the dance-play "Apollonius of Tyana," where he speaks of himself in speaking of Apollonius: "The problem is, how to extricate what he wants from the mess he is surrounded by, how to manage to locate what he himself feels."[6]

To come specifically to the formulation achieved in "The Kingfishers," we find, as the first item in the Storrs file, a prose note that is literally a preamble to the poem:

> The law is, to go to the heart of your time, to shoot for the core. And the only instrument is at the same time the material of it, which is the self. The old words on the stone at Delphi are correct, know thyself, but this extension of the principle, that the end of the knowing is the time, is the E hidden within the statement on the stone.

The constant danger is the narrows of the self, the natural narrows. Only the mind and the heart can keep a man free. This is true on the plane of perception. But on the plane of expression only form can do it, not personality. That is why the triumph is rare. It takes a mystery of both personality and form, to manage to shoot for the core and to hit it.

The danger is the very instrument itself, the self. For it must be used with an assurance of will, yet that very assurance leads to an assumption of self as power, and the confusion of the self with the truth.

What is the truth? It is nothing but the permanence of human effort shifting as it does its direction. Why it shifts is not so easy to say. Is it for as elementary and animal a reason as the simplest need of the nerves—for change? I should imagine this is a more accurate way to put it than we generally do when we talk of goals. They change. What does not change is the will to change

There is no period. When we turn over the page, we read the typed words:

What does not change / is the will to change

and two attempts at the opening stanzas of our poem. (See Appendix A.) I concur with Butterick's conclusion in his *American Poetry* article (p. 55): "We have, then, evidence as close to the actual moment of creation as we are ever likely to get in the critical study of a poem." He finds there "—not Neruda, not Heraclitus specifically, not any narrow Marxism or Prescott's Americanist history or amateur archeological yearnings—but deep thought over man's role in the universe." In other words, to have this record of how the poem came into being helps us to resolve some of the questions that have been associated with the first line.

The preceding prose passage is a political statement. Olson wants to extend the Delphic "Know thyself" to knowing one's time in order to take political action, "to shoot for the core and to hit it." Olson has not finished with this "human effort," although it shifts its course so unaccountably. Maybe there are laws for this shifting? The will to change, because of "the simplest need of the nerves," may be one of the laws. The passage stops far before settling any of the questions it raises. It stops at a one-line apercu, in which Olson feels he has expressed a pattern of history with accuracy and aplomb. So much so that he immediately wants to change gears and use it for the beginning of a poem:

> What does not change / is the will to change.

   The first thing to be said about this line is that an examination of its context within the prose passage should satisfy anyone that it is Olson's, not a borrowing. In saying that the "opening line is a translation of Heraclitus' Fragment 23," Guy Davenport was going beyond the bounds of probability in assuming Olson's Greek was as good as his own. He credits Olson with improvising an entirely new approach to Heraclitus's fragment: "Sensing in the etymology of *metabállon* the idea of wilfulness (*bállo*, I throw, is kin to *boúlomai*, I will), Olson translates *metabállon* as 'the will to change.'"[7] Butterick counters this proposition mildly in his *American Poetry* article (p. 56): "it is doubtful that the poet would have engaged in speculative translation from the Greek at that point." I think the prose passage proves that he didn't.

   The virgule (/) at the caesura of the line has prompted some queries. Pound used it as a form of punctuation, usually in connection with abbreviations. Olson, in the few places it occurs in his writings, uses it more as a musical beat, "a pause so light it hardly separates the words."[8] The opening line of "The Kingfishers," however, presents a unique situation. The virgule is a device we have for indicating a line break when we are quoting poetry within a prose essay. I think this is Olson's use of it here.

> What does not change / is the will to change.

It is as though the poet is saying: "I wrote a prose sentence that I immediately recognized as possibly two lines of poetry. I am going to use the sentence as the first line of my poem, typing it as it was in the prose piece, but using the slash mark to show that I feel it is really verse, and as verse would be two lines." If true, this move on the poet's part would be more impulsive than logical. But what seems to have been the desired effect is certainly achieved: the flatness of a prose statement with the feeling of measured verse. By this means, the heroics of the fateful telegram poem, "the K," was modulated into a topic sentence for a long political poem.

III

The prose preamble not only contains the first line of "The Kingfishers" but also the first line of part 2 of the poem:

> I thought of the E on the stone . . .

This takes us to one of the major sources for the poem, Plutarch's essay "On the E at Delphi." Olson bought his Bohn Classical Library copy of *Plutarch's Morals* in Washington in September 1948, a month before Peter Blanc's party. Because of his wife's miscarriage and slow convalescence, Olson could not work well at this time and bought books instead. "Constanza improves most slowly," he wrote to Edward Dahlberg on 20 September 1948.[9] "All I was able to do was to divert and prepare myself by buying Bohns and Loebs: Athenaeus, Hesiod, Catullus, the Anthology, the Morals, Theocritus, Herodotus, Percy's Reliques, John Lyly's Plays, Elizabethan Lyrics. I traded all week." Here is preparation for something. Back to basics. Soon after, he seems to have focused on Plutarch and the "important mystery" of the E at Delphi: Apollo implanted "in the knowledge-seeking part of the human soul an appetite that draws towards the truth; as is manifest from many other things, and from the dedication of the E."[10] Plutarch in a sort of Socratic dialogue goes through several of the proposed solutions to the mystery of the E. Olson ignores this rather fusty stuff, taking the E to be symbolic of the hidden part of the imperative, "Know thyself." This hidden part is, according to Olson's prose passage, an "extension of the principle" of knowing the self, which is that "the end of the knowing is the time." The "E hidden within the statement on the stone" is, then, for Olson, the imperative to know one's society as well as oneself.

If we apply this notion of "going to the heart of your time" to the poem's line 24—

> I thought of the E on the stone, and of what Mao said

—we deduce that the poet is not making a contrast between the E and Mao, but aligning them: to go to the heart of the time at the moment in history when "The Kingfishers" was being written is to come up against Mao, and what he represents, a new dawn in the East. E stands for East in the commonly accepted abbreviation. The "dawn" of civilization is again commonly accepted to be in the East, or Middle East. Delphi is "the womb among places." When Olson read those words in *Essays on a Science of Mythology*, he circled Kerenyi's insight that "it was a symbol of the uttermost beginning of things"[11] and wrote in the margin: "on the E at Delphi." Mao's China is in the East, or the Far East, and it represents a new beginning of things.

If Mao Tse-tung in "The Kingfishers" is a new Delphic oracle, how did Olson come to regard him in this light? The answer to that question leads first to the source for "what Mao said." Reading the passage in 1963 in Vancouver, Olson stopped to say: "That's Mao's report to the Chinese Communist Party in '48 that I'm using, two years before the taking of Peking. I read it in a French translation."[12]

> la lumiere . . .
> de l'aurore . . .
> est devant nous!
>
> . . . . .
>
> Mao concluded:
> nous devons
> nous lever
> et agir!
> (lines 25–29, 50–53)

George Butterick was able to find the exact source for the quotation in a letter from Jean Riboud to Olson, undated but about the end of 1948 (now at Storrs—see Butterick, p. 58). To understand the impression this letter made on Olson one should know that Riboud was a very special friend. "Has great eyes in his heart," Olson wrote of him to another friend, Ben Shahn. "Is one of the rare ones."[13] After Riboud visited the Olsons in Washington on 1 February 1949, this is what Olson wrote to Eleanor Melville Metcalf the next day (draft letter at Storrs):

A friend, a young banker, French, just back from France and here for a day on business with ERP, was here for dinner last night. We exchanged notes on the state of those provinces, France and the US. He expects a blood bath of a million Frenchmen soon and is so disgusted he plans to go back immediately in order to be there when it comes.

> For he knows there is no peace or war left (they too are dead) and a
> man must take on the generality as men once did the personal.

"Take on the generality"—another way of saying "go to the heart of your time." Riboud is teaching Olson by example that "know thyself" is just a step toward knowing the whole public arena. Riboud at this point was truly a man of the world. He was in Washington on behalf of the French-based Schlumberger Corporation and eventually became the chief executive officer of that most profitable of private corporations. Among Olson's friends, he is the only one to have had the right kind of fame for a "Profile" in *The New Yorker*, where we can find crucial facts of his life:[14]

> As a young man in Lyons, he flirted with Communism and railed against Franco, Fascism, and the French establishment, including the Roman Catholic Church. During the Second World War, he joined the Resistance;[15] he was captured in 1943 and sent to Buchenwald. Two years later, when he emerged, he had tuberculosis and weighed ninety-six pounds. . . . He speaks softly, sometimes almost inaudibly, in accented English, rarely gesticulates, and is an intense listener, usually inspecting his long fingers while others speak. Everything about Riboud conveys an impression of delicacy except his eyes, which are deep brown and cryptic.

Thanks to *The New Yorker* we can, as it were, look into the eyes of the person who asked Charles Olson to be best man at his wedding in October 1949, the person who had written to Olson a year previously about Mao Tse-tung's new dawn:

> Listen to this last sentence—It will wake you up in your sleep, it will strike you with a blow in your wandering day. I give it to you as my credo—
> "Voici l'ère historique dans laquelle le capitalisme modial et l'impérialisme vout vers leur condamnation, tandis que le socialisme modiale et la démocratie vout vers la victoire. La lumiere de l'aurore est devant nous. Nous devons nous lever et agir—"
> Don't lose it.
> Mao opened my eyes.[16]

I do not think it diminishes the poem to discover that Mao's words did not come to Olson via official dispatches. It is all the more moving that a dear friend, this particular friend, provided by letter another *given* for "The Kingfishers" as an act within *l'univers concentrationaire:*

> nous devons
> > nous lever
> > > et agir!

IV

To introduce Mao favorably into a poem in 1949 "was actually a bold position to take," Butterick notes in an informed comment: "The powerful anti-Communist 'China Lobby' in the United States was out riding and would soon come down hard on China experts such as Olson's acquaintance Owen Lattimore for alleged communist sympathies, almost upending his life and certainly dislocating his career" (p. 40). One person who helped Olson have the confidence to be pro-China was Robert Payne, who had been to visit Mao in Yenan. Payne went to China in 1942 and spent the whole war studying Chinese literature and history at the evacuated universities in Chungking. One of the results of these years, his anthology of Chinese poetry, the well-known *The White Pony*, had just been published and was a topic of discussion when Olson and Payne met in Hollywood in September 1947.[17] Not long after, Payne sent Olson his just published survey of the nationalistic movements of the Far East, entitled *The Revolt of Asia*. The letter Olson wrote in response to it is lost, but there are several indirect allusions to its thesis in, for instance, "Notes for the Proposition: Man is Prospective," where Olson echoes Payne in speaking of "the persisting failure to count what Asia will do to collectivism, the mere quantities of her people leverage enough to move the earth, leaving aside the moral grace of such of her leaders as Nehru, Mao, Shjarir."[18] These named leaders were ones that Payne had written about in the humane way that was typical of him. If Olson felt at all close to Mao and could place him in "The Kingfishers" as a felt personage, it was probably due to Payne's giving Olson that sense of Mao in his writings and conversation.[19]

Let us state unequivocally, then, that at the core of "The Kingfishers" is the issue of politics, and cite Olson's very first comment we have on the poem, which is in a letter to Payne of 24 February

1949: "I am locked in what looks like my first long poem and what is my first attempt to grapple with the issue." The context for this remark is that Payne had asked if he could dedicate to the Olsons his new book *The Tormentors*, a novel set in a Soviet penal camp. Olson cannot accept. "For on this issue I am either very very timid or, what I suppose is the same thing, very very shrewd," he writes in reply. "And in politics (which again looks up, now that my gang wrung Acheson, at least, out of the mess) I play like any American—a poker player." He was perhaps taking the responsibility of being a dedicatee too seriously, but he never did sign petitions or allow his name to be used in support of causes. "I purchase any statement I am able to make a propos society only after the gravest labor," he explained to Payne. "I only know where I stand when I have arrived there thus torturously." He mentions "the Pound piece" as an example, which "was months in the making." The contortions Olson went through in the drafts that led up to "This is Yeats Speaking"[20] confirm what difficulty Olson had *as a writer* in facing the political issue that Pound's actions had posed. As a back-room politician he would have known in real-politic terms what to do that was possible to do; however, the duty to be scrupulously moral in words, within the *polis* of his fellow writers, left Olson almost tongue-tied. He ended up not speaking in his own voice, but using the persona of W. B. Yeats, surveying Pound in chains from the lofty height of old-world values. The aim is perspective and sensitivity, but the result is not entirely successful. Three years later he is still seeking the proper distance and voice, to view the world as a whole and tell the truth about it.

Referring to the ending of Chaucer's *Troilus and Criseyde*, Olson felt that he should "seek Troilus' vantage, to try to see our time at one glance as he did the earth from the seventh sphere, regard its motions and say, swiftly, where it tends." This quotation is from the previously cited "Notes for the Proposition: Man is Prospective," which can be dated around 11 May 1948. By July 1948 Olson had written a "mask" called *Troilus*, confirming that he was less interested in the tortured lover than this final Troilus who can see everything clearly, like the astronaut Yuri Gagarin, "the only man, so far as I know, who ever got a look at the whole world over his shoulder in one glance."[21]

But Olson has to acknowledge that his own vantage ought to be better than Troilus's after "100 years of analysis into the ways of man and universe." The "Notes for the Proposition: Man is Prospective" lists a series of names associated with modern scientific thought and psychology: Marx, Darwin, Renan, Fourier, Sorel, Frazer, Freud, Spengler, Kierkegaard, Einstein, De Sitter, and Frobenius: these should be "enough to go on." He reckons that if Troilus had seen these motions on earth he would have recognized "a direction as profound as the change of attention which we call the Renaissance." He has to move from a perception of what needs to be done to the job of doing it. He can readily use the word "Renaissance" in a prescriptive essay, but can he get the "way" of this new Renaissance into the form it ought to be? He suspects that "the place to find synthesis is not in politics, science or religions but the arts."[22] He wrote to his friend Henry Murray on 20 July 1948 about this essay: "I don't think the form is right, think now it better be verse eventually, if it is anything" (letter at Storrs). "The Kingfishers" is the poem that he told Payne on 24 February 1949 was his first attempt "to grapple with the issue"—and he really meant the whole view of things. He will know where he stands when he has "arrived there thus torturously." All this talk, he is saying in effect, had better lead to a major poem of political health, one that is destructive enough, one that is itself an example of fresh growth.

3

Modes of Form

I

Olson's "Projective Verse" essay was written a year after "The Kingfishers." There is a fit between the two of them that seems to confirm what we might suspect, that the essay is describing the kind of poetry-making he had just done, as he perceived it. So, using the wording of "Projective Verse," we can see "The Kingfishers" as "energy transferred from where the poet got it (he will have some several causations), by way of the poem itself to, all the way over to, the reader . . . a high energy-construct and, at all points, an energy-discharge."[1] In other words, the poem is a communication from poet to reader, a communication by means of language that has received heightened energy of expression from the particular nature of the several subjects the poem has been asked to carry and that has the strength to deposit that energy with like intent with the reader. The key phrase is "he will have some several causations." This translates into the first axiom of projective verse: "Form is never more than an extension of content" (*Selected Writings*, p. 16). You have something to say, you have the energy to say it, and the form follows. You eschew any traditional container for this individual power-speech.

If we take this principle into an examination of the form of "The Kingfishers," we can see it as a way of understanding what happened when the "What does not change is the will to change" of the prose preamble stopped him short. The energy the author felt at that moment required it to be discharged as a verse line, and so it proceeded to be. One cannot perhaps put a name to the causation that made the poet immediately turn to the birds and the Fernand episode, but clearly the narrative form is determined by the anecdotal content. What follows in the poem will be the result of the questions implicit in the anecdote: what kind of forces were at work at Angkor Vat and what does this specific case say about history as a whole?

If the poem as it moves into part 2 does not strike one as answering an asked question, then it will probably be because of the second axiom of projective verse: "One perception must immediately and directly lead to a further perception" (*Selected Writings*, p. 17). This is a matter of aesthetics. The traditional graces of syntactical communication might sometimes be set aside to gain a better coefficiency of drag: "get on with it, keep moving, keep in, speed, the nerves, their speed, the perceptions, theirs, the acts, the split second acts, the whole business, keep it moving as fast as you can" (*Selected Writings*, p. 17). "The Kingfishers" reflects the poet's life as it was then: fast, living on his nerves, with the urgency to be of use. "Projective Verse" is telling us that, as readers of the poem, we have to jump to it. We cannot expect to be coached. Without customary signposts, we have to see, for instance, that the juxtaposition of Mao and the kingfishers is what the poem requires as a follow-on to part 1.

> I thought of the E on the stone, and of what Mao said
> la lumiere"
>   but the kingfisher
> de l'aurore"
>   but the kingfisher flew west
> est devant nous!
>   he got the color of his breast
>   from the heat of the setting sun!
>
>   (lines 24–31)

This, in contrasting images, is the beginning of a discussion of the rise and fall of empires, of which process Angkor Vat is an instance, and America and China are current instances. The form follows the content: the idea of the rising East contrasting with the setting West suggests the balanced half-lines. And so it goes.

Perhaps there is a touch of the ornamental in the preceding lines, a leaning toward the aesthetically attractive (even a rhyme!), which might have caused Olson to interrupt his Vancouver 1963 reading of the poem at this point to say, "I like that

contrast of this shove as against the kingfisher." Nothing else was
said: it may be more of an apology than a pat on the back. In the
poem, he makes sure to defuse any possible prettiness by moving
on to what amounts to an encyclopedia entry. He had already
incorporated a detail from his old workhorse, *The Encyclopaedia
Britannica*, in the lines about the kingfisher's breast: "originally
a plain grey bird it acquired its present bright colours by flying
towards the sun on its liberation from Noah's ark, when its upper
surface assumed the hue of the sky above it and its lower plumage
was scorched by the heat of the setting orb to the tint it now
bears."[2] In his picking up this piece of medieval science, Olson is
being positively euphuistic.[3] If we were talking about metaphysical
poetry, we would call it a conceit, a detail that with some
ingenuity carries forward the theme of the poem. After this, Olson
feels it is time to turn to the ingenuous, or the apparently so,
presenting in lines 32–35 a flat zoological description from the
encyclopedia:

> The features are, the feebleness of the feet (syndactylism of the 3rd
>   & 4th digit)
> the bill, serrated, sometimes a pronounced beak, the wings
> where the color is, short and round, the tail
> inconspicuous.

This can be compared with the *Encylcopaedia Britannica* passage
from which it came:

> One of their most remarkable features is the feebleness of their feet,
> and the union (syndactylism) of the third and fourth digits. . . . In
> most forms the bill does not differ much from that of the common
> *Alcedo ispida*, but in *Syma* its edges are serrated, while in *Carcineutes, Dacelo* and *Melidora* the maxilla is prolonged, becoming in
> the last a very pronounced hook. Generally the wings are short and
> rounded, and the tail is in many forms inconspicuous.

Any discrepancies between this entry and the poem are insignificant,
or at any rate are not damaging to our sense of this passage
as scientific description. As Olson says later in the poem, at line
111: "We can be precise." The poem is an investigation into how
well we can know things. There is the problem of change—what
can we know of its causes? Take Angkor Vat and its kingfishers—

3: Modes of Form

what happened? We can examine the birds themselves in detail. "But not these things were the factors. Not the birds" (line 36). We can, of course, discount the legends, which are after all merely legends.

> The legends are
> legends. Dead, hung up indoors, the kingfisher
> will not indicate a favoring wind,
> or avert the thunderbolt. Nor, by its nesting,
> still the waters, with the new year, for seven days
>
> (lines 37–41)

Again, the *Encyclopaedia Britannica* (p. 808):

> the kingfisher was supposed to possess many virtues. Its dried body would avert thunderbolts . . . or hung by a thread to the ceiling of a chamber would point with its bill to the quarter whence the wind blew . . . All readers of Ovid (Metam. bk. xi.) know how . . . all gales were hushed and the sea calmed so that their floating nest might ride uninjured over the waves during the seven proverbial "Halcyon days."

And more:

> Very early in the year it prepares its nest, which is at the end of a tunnel bored by itself in a bank, and therein the six or eight white, glossy, translucent eggs are laid, sometimes on the bare soil, but often on the fishbones which, being indigestible, are thrown up in pellets by the birds; and, in any case, before incubation is completed these *rejectamenta* accumulate so as to form a pretty cup-shaped structure that increases in bulk after the young are hatched, but, mixed with their fluid excretions and with decaying fishes brought for their support, soon becomes a dripping fetid mass.

Which gives us lines 42–49 of the poem:

> It is true, it does nest with the opening year, but not on the waters.
> It nests at the end of a tunnel bored by itself in a bank. There,
> six or eight white and translucent eggs are laid, on fishbones
> not on bare clay, on bones thrown up in pellets by the birds.
>   On these rejectamenta
> (as they accumulate they form a cup-shaped structure) the young
>   are born.

> And, as they are fed and grow, this nest of excrement and decayed fish becomes a dripping, fetid mass.

I suggest that something quite unexpected has happened here. After saying that it must be something other than the kingfishers that are the factors of change, as the poem picks up momentum entirely from the factual vitality of its source's language it seems to be rejecting that proposition. It seems to be building up an indictment of birds that find a "dripping, fetid" nest all right to live in. If the kingfisher's breast and the setting sun, put in contrast with Mao, symbolize declining Western Civilization, then the stinking nest perforce becomes an image of neglect and perfidy, society fouling its own cities and farmland. If this were not true, how could we feel so positive a relief at Mao's words, as they cut into the description of the "dripping, fetid mass"?

> Mao concluded:
> nous devons
> nous lever
> et agir!
>
> (lines 50–53)

We must raise ourselves up and act! It is ourselves who are at fault. Civilizations have more to fear from their own internal laziness and corruption than any external enemy. Mao is cleaning out the fetid nest of China. Are we going to clean out ours or simply die like Angkor Vat?

Did Olson know, when he started documenting the qualities of the kingfisher from his encyclopedia, that it would lead him to such an image of decay and move the poem into such a space that Mao can properly end part 2 as he began it? The answer would probably be no. The poet is almost like a master of ceremonies at the occasion of the poem; he "recognizes" what comes next. In part 2 the words "It is true" of line 42 record a change of tone, the expectation of a new movement in the poem, a recognition that something is about to happen. It is such a thing that "Projective Verse" is trying to convey by the word "recognition" in the pertinent passage below (*Selected Writings*, p. 20):

> The objects which occur at every given moment of composition (of recognition, we can call it) are, can be, must be treated exactly as

they do occur therein and not by any ideas or preconceptions from outside the poem, must be handled as a series of objects in field in such a way that a series of tensions (which they also are) are made to *hold*, and to hold exactly inside the content and the context of the poem which has forced itself, through the poet and them, into being.

According to this concept, the poem itself forces into being a form each instant of its ongoing. It is as though the poet was being used by the poem to shape the materials of its universe. Thus torturously.

II

We did not quote swathes of *Encyclopaedia Britannica* to prove that Olson can accurately transcribe passages into his poem, but to meet the terms of a full explication. It illustrates one of Olson's basic modes of form, the inclusion of primary documents. "It is a matter, finally, of OBJECTS," says "Projective Verse," "what they are, what they are inside a poem, how they got there, and, once there, how they are to be used" (*Selected Writings*, p. 20). In this context, what could be more prized as an "object" than factual document free of the stain of subjective handling? "A Bibliography on America for Ed Dorn" is a 1955 guidebook, from teacher to student at Black Mountain College, on methodology for putting oneself in a position to write about America. Olson there lays great stress on primary documents, including manuscript archives:

And to hook on here is a lifetime of assiduity. Best thing to do is to *dig one thing or place or man* until you yourself know more abt that than is possible to any other man. It doesn't matter whether it's Barbed Wire or Pemmican or Paterson or Iowa. But *exhaust* it. Saturate it. Beat it.
　　　　　　　　　　　　And then U KNOW everything else very fast: one saturation job (it might take 14 years). And you're in, forever. (*Additional Prose*, p. 11)

Olson had done his saturation job with Melville, exactly fourteen years from beginning his master's thesis to finishing *Call Me Ishmael*. So he did not have to do it again for something like kingfishers. He would know already the kind of effort with primary research that would have gone into, for instance, an authoritative encyclopedia entry. His assiduous nose would tell him immediately how authentic it was and thus available for use, as part of the given, part of the truth of the poem.

It is in this regard that Pound as a model was important. The *Cantos* paved the way for Olson to write poems containing lots of quotation. This is obvious, and no more needs to be said on this point. What is disputable is whether or not Olson's use of quotations is like Pound's. Pound's was the method of "luminous details"—or luminous clumps in some Cantos—which are defined by Hugh Kenner in *The Pound Era* (University of California, 1971) as "patterned integrities" that "transferred out of their context of origin retain their power to enlighten us" (p. 153). Such a luminous detail is the column in San Zeno signed by its maker, put to use by Pound in his *usura* cantos (Kenner, pp. 324–326). Luminous details are most often found constelled with others, this conjunctivity making a point that would normally require a denotative sentence or explanation (e.g., usury does not have to be defined when it is exposed in the images of its effects contrasted with images of a healthy financial state). The combination of different images to produce a desired concept spatially rather than syntactically was termed an "ideogram," drawing on Ernest Fenollosa's work, which Pound edited as *The Chinese Written Character as a Medium for Poetry*. Rudimentary ideographs (or word signs derived from pictures of the thing denoted) are put together in Chinese to produce a more complex idea, as the sign for "a man" put beside the sign for "word" gives us "sincerity" (i.e., a man standing by his word) (Kenner, p. 227). Olson originally read Fenollosa in 1945 because of Pound, but had his own take on it, as Creeley noticed: "I don't think even Ez, who I've read, certainly with all possible attention, can be called as direct, in his continuance, as you have been on this matter. I wd now say, if anyone's you are F/s son, i.e., this is the man behind you, the one who lights up yr own word" (letter of 29 September 1951, *Creeley Correspondence* 7, pp. 207–208). In a letter of 18 November 1951, Olson concurred that "my interest in Fenollosa is, as you have pointed out, to some clear degree at root a different interest than Ez's" (*Creeley Correspondence*, 8, p. 150). In a later letter (*Creeley Correspondence* 10, pp. 63–64) he talks of Pound's "misuse" of Fenollosa and ideogram and how it "rankles": "by using them however improperly, he has harmed them." These are mere hints: it would take a great deal of sifting and thinking to fathom what is being said here. At the moment we can only speculate that Olson felt the ideogram was essentially static, a patterned gerund at best. What he saw in Fenollosa was a far cry from this: the active principle of the motion inherent in nouns. He mentions Fenollosa once in "Projective Verse," in criticizing Hart Crane for his continual "push to the nominative": "there is a loss in Crane of what Fenollosa is so right about, in syntax, the sentence as first act of nature, as lightning, as passage of force from subject to object, quick, in this case, from Hart to me, in every case, from me to you, the VERB, between two nouns" (*Selected Writings*, p. 21). We should not go too far afield. Suffice it to say, on this evidence, that Olson feels he is not at all ideogrammatic in his methodology.

We can better get at the issue by returning to "The Kingfishers," part 2. Guy Davenport, a Poundian, found that it comprised three ideogrammatic elements: "All three ideogrammatic elements are held in a relation to the sun: the Delphi stone religiously, Mao metaphorically and rhetorically, the kingfisher mythically" (p. 254). If this were true, it would make a pretty heliotype, where differences are fused into one white light. The ideogrammatic mind is interested in equivalences, and has the satisfaction of finding them almost everywhere. I cannot myself imagine any satisfaction resulting from trying to see Delphi, Mao, and the kingfisher as equivalent in relation to the sun. I begin to suspect that Davenport may be taking some delight in establishing that "The Kingfishers" as a Poundian poem is not a very good one. It is true that it is not a good Poundian poem; it is not a Poundian poem at all. It is discursive, not ideogrammatic.

It is my belief that the ideogrammatic method did not stand Pound in very good stead. He had some things to say. In his prose he got them said. But turning to the writing of the *Cantos*, Pound chose *expression* over *communication*. I borrow these terms from the same Olson letter in which he says Pound's misuse "of Fenollosa, of ideogram does rankle" (*Creeley Correspondence* 10, p. 63). They occur further down the page; Olson does not apply them to Pound. I think he could have. He says "that the dimension of any act is the amount of desire in it to communicate and that expression is not the same drive, is somehow inevitably short of the demand." It is the job of artists "not to express themselves but to communicate." We do not have to settle the issue as regards Pound. Olson may not have been thinking about Pound, but we may be sure he was thinking of himself. His self-prescriptive mode of operation: to communicate.

III

It might explain something about "The Kingfishers" to know that at the time "awkwardness" was for Olson a critical term with positive connotations. He admired the "awkwardness" of Sienese painting, as opposed to the usually more favored Florentine.

> Awkwardness, the grace
> the absence of the suave.[4]

Thus begins the poem "Siena," written soon after Olson returned from the Democratic Party Convention in Philadelphia 12–16 July 1948. It was a symbolic act, the last gasp of that kind, to "rub myself against the beast of politics and see my fur rise," as he put it to Henry Murray in a letter of 20 July 1948. But there was another symbolic act: "In Philadelphia I went, for the first time, to the Museum, and this Giovanni startled me again. . . . I guess it turns out he's one of my fated ones. . . . At least he stands as an oppose, for us, I think, to the suavity of art and spirit, as much in our time as in the Renaissance that followed him." This is Giovanni di Paolo (1402–1482), whom he goes on to contrast with Picasso ("competence and quantity"): "It is G di P's awkwardness that holds a value for us, an awkwardness I'm tempted to think is permanently the clothes of the spirit." Not to have to be suave is very liberating; to be offered the insight that one's old awkwardness is true grace is freedom indeed. One is no longer hooked on beauty. This may be what is behind Olson's remark from the platform at Berkeley when he said, reacting to a refrain in Cantos 74 and 80, "we're here to say something a hell of a lot more important than 'beauty is difficult'" (*Muthologos* 1, p. 121).

It had been Giovanni's "Saint Clare Saving a Ship in Distress," brought to Washington with the "Paintings from the Berlin Museum" exhibition March-April 1948, which had first struck him and started this deep reevaluation. In the painting, the figure of St. Clare hovering above the storm-battered ship was without legs. It was a kind of reality Olson felt he had not encountered before. It reinforced an instinct Olson had for modest individuality, going back to his father—"mediocre humanitas" is the phrase he used in this connection in a Storrs notebook of 8 March 1948. "There is simply the literal essence and exactitude of your own," he said, trying to sum up this quality in 1965: "I mean, the streets you live on, or the clothes you wear, or the color of your hair is no different from the ability of, say, Giovanni di Paolo to cut the legs off Santa Clara." He concluded, "Truth lies solely in what you do with it."[5]

If "The Kingfishers" sometimes seems like a poem with its legs cut off it will have the blessing of Giovanni di Paolo. Truth takes the guise of awkwardness, as lies are covered over by suavity. Olson told Caresse Crosby in a letter of 23 July 1948 that, after Philadelphia, he wanted to write about Giovanni. "The coins I'm handling, the counters, are: awkwardness (as permanent cloth of spirit), the oblique as a via to confront direct—as guerillas, maquis—the enemy. The enemy being: quantity, materialism, the suave." Then, to bring the whole thing back to current politics, he names the name that for him typifies the suave—none other than "Chiang Kai Check," the enemy.[6]

IV

It should be clear that part 2 of "The Kingfishers" is an answer to the "why" of part 1—or the beginning of an answer. "I thought of. . . . But not these were the factors. . . . It is true. . . ." This is the procedure of puzzling through some problem. The beginning of part 3 is a more direct answer and would have come immediately after the question if the poem had followed the first plan as indicated by prose notes on an early worksheet in the "Kingfisher" file at Storrs:

The features are, the feebleness of their feet, with syndactylism of the third and fourth digit, the bill, sometimes serrated, sometimes a very pronounced hook, the wings short and round, the tail inconspicuous. But not these things were the factors. What were? Was is a change of attention on the part of their keepers, or a sudden cold? How did the jungle suddenly leap in, more swiftly than the kingfishers dive?

Part 3 of the poem begins:

> When the attentions change / the jungle
> leaps in
>   even the stones are split
>   they rive.
>   (lines 54–57)

After the intervention of part 2 (just to be "awkward"), we now have what even composition courses might call a "topic sentence": a bio-economic regional disaster can occur with the change of society's focus. However, this kind of fatal inattentiveness is a danger we fear less than a conflict-triggered holocaust. Rightly so, on the presumption that human nature tends more to violence than transcendental meditation:

> Or,
> enter
> that other conqueror we more naturally recognize
> he so resembles ourselves.
>   (lines 58–61)

Mr. Cortez.

There is a logicality in the use of history here that resembles Hart Crane's *The Bridge* as much as it does anything else in modern poetry. A "bridge" is a way of getting into history, and *The Bridge* uses numerous jumping off points: Columbus, Pocahontas, Depression railroad bums, a prairie pioneer mother, and closest to home, the Brooklyn Bridge. Crane was impatient with the "history primer" type of chronology: "What I am after," he wrote in a letter, "is an assimilation of this experience, a more organic panorama, showing the continuous and living evidence of the past in the inmost vital substance of the present."[7] It is not known that Olson had seen this statement of Crane's at this time, but "The Kingfishers" indicates that he would have understood it perfectly.

Olson once told Creeley that he had "the sense that crane and bill [williams] are more naturally of my predecession than some others [i.e., pound]" (letter 20 August 1951, *Creeley Correspondence* 7, p. 110). His engagement with Hart Crane goes back further than with Williams. He quoted Crane's poem "At Melville's Tomb" as epigraph to his M.A. thesis in 1933. His first poem, his first presentable poem, was an elegy for Crane, "Birth's Obituary" of 1940 (recast and retitled "You, Hart Crane"), which begins, in its earliest version:

> Plane's flight your helix, . . .
> . . . .
> New Archeopteryx, you Hart Crane
> Flew where others falter.[8]

The archeopteryx was the oldest known bird that has been found in fossil form. Bird motif again. The trouble was that Crane was a bird that was always soaring above and away from a factual historical base. "What still bothers me," Olson wrote to Creeley of Crane (*Creeley Correspondence* 7, p. 114), "is, the *lifting*—the allowing the phrase to *rise*—instead . . . of *pointering* and then, instantly, *because there is so much*, pushing on." Olson's point would be that Crane was always trying to conjure the American spirit to rise from the American earth through a frenzied dance. He could not resist the allure of creating beauty out of conquest.

Olson cooled it by going to document. No heroics allowed, not even the intellectual apotheosis of the Frontier Theory. Olson was going to fight the allure by means of William Prescott's unrelenting *History of the Conquest of Mexico*. It was way too late for Crane's glamorizing. He wanted to tell Crane that "already the body of this land was crocked" (*Creeley Correspondence* 1, p. 144). By 1941 Prescott had shown Olson in detail how America came to be "crocked." Crane seemed to know it but refused to accept it; the strain showed in his high style. The two poets are similar in having each a thesis about American history, but in the end there is an opposite effect. Crane strove with concentrations of brilliant imagery for a romantic ideal, until strain turned to exhaustion. Olson did not work at it so hard, used sources and authorities like a debater, and sometimes faltered where Crane would no doubt have flown. But Olson worked hard enough, made his points one way or another, and produced what Alan C. Golding has called "perhaps the first major essay-poem since Pope's 'Essay on Man.'"[9]

V

That the young Charles Olson was good at writing essays there can be no doubt. Wilbert Snow, his English professor at Wesleyan, was so impressed with the Yeats paper Olson did as an undergraduate that he never threw it out, and it can now be perused in the Snow papers in Wesleyan Library.[10] It is a polemical argument for Yeats's early romantic poetry as against the later "modern" Yeats! Stressing Celtic myth and mysticism, this essay is a small premonition of Olson turning his back on the modern to seek a postmodern in archaic survivals and alternative presences.

One particular Yeats quotation jumped out at him: "Public speaking is the best school of exactness for a writer." Olson says it "warmed" him to read these words.[11] They were a confirmation of many years of effort on Olson's part. He distinguished himself in high school as an orator, winning regional public-speaking contests and finishing third in the national championship (the prize took him to Europe for the summer of 1928). Now at Wesleyan he was becoming a star debater. In all, he participated in eight intercollegiate debates and lost on only one occasion. He won against Vassar with the resolve that censorship should be abolished; he won against Yale, negating the proposition that there should be federal compulsory unemployment insurance; he won against Princeton on the negative side of the topic that "education in patriotism should not be encouraged"; he won against Oberlin, this time in favor of enacting unemployment insurance; he won against Williams, debating that the Soviet Union should not be recognized; he won against Lafayette and Amherst.[12] These were all exercises in persuasiveness. "The Kingfishers" strikes one as being within that same genre.

If so, if Olson in the poem is exercising his skills as a debater, doing what he can do best, what then is the proposition being debated? Might it have something to do with that old chestnut, progress? Olson's first freshman essay was entitled "Progress." Americans pride themselves on being progressive, but in his European tour that summer he felt that America could learn a lot from Europe about "true progress, the progress of civilization."[13] At Storrs there exists a page of notes for a talk Olson gave on 7 January 1931 to students at Middletown High School (most of whom must have been at least three years younger than him). The college Junior spoke on the subject "Things That Never Change." He covered everything: Literature, Art, Theatre, Religion, and for the last topic dealt with "Progress." What exactly he said we do not know, but I think it must have been the proposition: "What does not change is the will to change."

One more example, from the two-year stint Olson did as a instructor in English at Clark University in his hometown of Worcester, where he spoke at an antiwar rally on 13 November 1935.

> Probably the outstanding contribution of the day was the speech delivered by Professor Charles Olson, in which he pointed out the inherent barbarism in man, the emotional forces that drove men into battle—ending with the warning that only by substituting a cause with as great an emotional appeal as war, only by fighting war with the fanaticism of religious maniacs, could the peacemakers hope to avert war, even temporarily.[14]

More could be cited. Olson developed techniques of persuasion, success bred success, and he could not stop being a debater—at least, had not stopped by the time he wrote "The Kingfishers."

Perhaps, indeed, the form of the poem has something to do with the kind of performance Olson expected of himself as a debater—as he described it in a college notebook (now at Storrs):

> It is at once an aid and handicap that my style of debating depends on my mental exhilaration. I hate to prepare formal arguments—and frequently I speak muddleheadedly. But if the pistons of my mind are firing properly, as today, then logic and conviction and fluency is mine. Usually the exhilaration of a formal debate steps my mind up enough to ensure success.[15]

There was some muddleheadedness along the way in the composition of the poem, as we shall see. For a long time in the gestation Olson did not know he had twins (he landed the other one, "The Praises," safely too eventually). But there would be a day when the mental exhilaration was there; the pistons were working; and, therefore, what we can look for in "The Kingfishers" is just what he knows he has to give: "logic and conviction and fluency."

VI

A substantial assertion may find a way to get itself said through the passionate haphazardness of a well-trained mind. Olson was early influenced by a statement of Melville's that begins chapter 82 of *Moby-Dick*: "There are some enterprises in which a careful disorderliness is the true method." Quoting this in his master's thesis (p. 125), Olson underlined for emphasis the word "careful." His thesis was extremely careful, amazing only in the size of the job he took on. It took Edward Dahlberg in the years 1936–38 to shake him out of his well-behaved prose style; then it took until the end of the war for him to spring himself from Edward Dahlberg's style, and write *Call Me Ishmael* as his own.

It was apparently seeing what Sergei Eisenstein had done in his films "Alexander Nevsky" (1938) and "Ivan the Terrible" (1944) that gave Olson the license to finish his Melville book with "careful disorderliness." In an interview Olson stated that Eisenstein was "the one man in the world" who was "the measure" for his new methodology: "what I was trying to do in *Ishmael* was to put together—see, I won't use that word 'montage,' which we could use if we talk about Eisenstein. But, in fact, what Eisenstein was doing was . . . *convertere*, which means 'to turn together.'" (*Muthologos* 2, pp. 94, 103). To fellow-Melvillean Jay Leyda, Olson wrote of the "graphic-dramatic method" in *Call Me Ishmael*, which "makes juxtaposition possible" (letter dated 4 February 1946, carbon copy at Storrs). Olson knew Leyda would understand, being a particular friend of Eisenstein's and the editor of the English translations of his books. Olson undoubtedly had seen a copy of *The Film Sense* (New York, 1947) prior to finishing "The Kingfishers," where he could have read such passages as the following:

> our films are faced with the task of presenting not only a narrative that is *logically connected*, but one that contains a *maximum of emotion and stimulating power*. Montage is a mighty aid in the resolution of this task . . . juxtaposition of two separate shots by splicing them

together resembles not so much a simple sum of one shot plus another shot—as it does a *creation*. . . . Each montage-piece had a double responsibility—to build the *total line* as well as to continue the movement within *each of the contributory themes*.[16]

Montage can be used stupidly, which is perhaps why Olson did not want to use the term. A *fluid* montage, juxtapositions that further a theme by *convertere*, a "turning together," this is what we do find in "The Kingfishers." Eisenstein did not live to see the poem, but when Leyda forwarded a copy of *Call Me Ishmael*, Eisenstein acknowledged his mutual recognition with a telegram.[17]

V

Olson made one mistake of oversimplification when in the "Projective Verse" essay he started talking about the typewriter as a way of "scoring" verse lines on the page, saying it was time to pick "the fruits of the experiments of Cummings" (*Selected Writings*, p. 22). After listening to Cummings at the Institute of Contemporary Arts in Washington on 21 November 1950, Olson changed his mind about "this man who was so long poet to me" (*Creeley Correspondence* 4, p. 41). He now considered Cummings and his techniques "uninventive." That is how people soon came to see the whole business of composition by typewriter in "Projective Verse." Weak-brained critics, when all else in Olson was beyond them, were pleased to have this to ridicule. It was a too careful orderliness, but I'm sure Olson was not proposing to bring constraint to open verse. What he wanted to emphasize by talking about the typewriter as an aid to formal presentation was its potential use as "the personal and instantaneous recorder of the poet's work" as "the sons of Pound and Williams" were already practicing it, where the ear was the "measurer" and "the intervals of its composition" could be put down on the page with fidelity to the energy of the poet's breath-line (*Selected Writings*, p. 23). Olson was thinking about how best to take a snapshot of birds on the wing. He said it better in a letter to Frances Boldereff of 16 January 1950:

> the problem of a poem (that which explains the coming into existence of form) is, that it stay within itself. Not spill out, and, likewise, that

it contain all that it has to contain. This is the struggle. And it is permanently difficult, is new each time, and defies any law other than the new one each new one creates. And the only clue is rhythm, which is only to be described as the force and use of, the discipline of, the individual who has listened, and wants, at the moment he or she writes draws hammers shapes, to speak.

"Projective Verse" only slipped up when it tried with the typewriter business to be prescriptively specific. On the whole, its effect was a great act of liberation for all poets who were ready for it, mainly because it was vague enough to be useful.

Because of this healthy vagueness there is a limit to its applicability to any individual poem, even the one that closely preceded it. "The Kingfishers" was projective, but only in its own way. "It is history," Olson wrote to Boldereff (letter of 26 June 1950), and its method of composition is not "a viable method" for anything other than its "own kind of material." No theory of general prosody is going to adequately describe what is going on in it. Olson laid the problem out with one simple illustration in an unpublished letter to Creeley (2 April 1953 at Stanford Library), saying that with "The Kingfishers" a "non-accentual (quantitative) line has been returned into the language": "That is, 'syndactylism of the 3rd & 4th digit' won't, for me, scan. At the same time it ain't prose. But if it ain't prose . . . those birds will have to face up to this non-music as in there, in verse, and not to be got out." Olson leaves us birds with this problem. We accept it. His verse is what it is. We don't need a literary theory before we can look at a poem.

4
Recurrences

I

I am able to bring to the explication of part 3 of "The Kingfishers" a unique resource, Olson's own marked copy of William Prescott's *History of the Conquest of Mexico*, which recently became available for study.[1] With some satisfaction we can turn to pages 196–97 of this Modern Library edition and see the poet's double pencil lines in the margin against Prescott's footnote listing the treasures surrendered by Montezuma to Cortez. For the record, the phrases of the footnote that are pertinent to lines 69–81 of the poem can be excerpted:

> Two birds made of green feathers, with feet, beaks, and eyes of gold,—and, in the same piece with them, animals of gold, resembling snails. . . . A large wheel of gold, with figures of strange animals on it, and worked with tufts of leaves; weighing three thousand, eight hundred ounces. . . . Two birds made of thread and feather-work having the quills of their wings and tails, their feet, eyes, and the ends of their beaks of gold,—standing upon two reeds covered with gold, which are raised on balls of feather-work and gold embroidery, one white and the other yellow, with seven tassels of feather-work hanging from each of them.

This becomes, in part 3 of the poem:

>   "of green feathers   feet, beaks and eyes
>   of gold
>
>   "animals likewise,
>   resembling snails

> "a large wheel, gold, with figures of unknown four-foots,
> and worked with tufts of leaves, weight
> 3800 ounces
>
> "last, two birds, of thread and featherwork, the quills
> gold, the feet
> gold, the two birds perched on two reeds
> gold, the reeds arising from two embroidered mounds,
> one yellow, the other
> white.
>   "And from each reed hung
>   seven feathered tassels.
>
> (lines 69–81)

There is a notable emphasis in Olson's selection of items on feathers and gold. Birds as a theme is not going to last in the poem. It does not have primary organizational force. But if we see a connection back to Angkor Vat, we discover a neatness, as far as it goes, in the association of the Indo-Chinese kingfishers and the artificial birds of Aztec jewelry. They might both be taken as signifying the sensate end of an era.

For Olson does not—no more than Prescott—glamorize the Aztec empire. The priests are far from attractive:

> In this instance, the priests
> (in dark cotton robes, and dirty,
> their dishevelled hair matted with blood, and flowing wildly
> over their shoulders)
> rush in among the people, calling on them
> to protect their gods.
>
> (lines 84–89)

Make no mistake: these are Montezuma's priests. The passage is underlined in Prescott (p. 194):

> The Indian warriors gathered from all quarters, with shrill cries and clashing of weapons; while the priests, in their dark cotton robes, with dishevelled tresses matted with blood, flowing wildly over their shoulders, rushed frantic among the natives, calling upon them to protect their gods from violation!

4: Recurrences

Equally unexpected, perhaps, is the fact that Cortez's brutality is nowhere directly pictured in the poem. The underlinings in Prescott indicate that Olson read practically every word, and could have used innumerable passages to put Cortez in a bad light, but he remained mute. The poem is not going out of its way to engage our emotions on heroes and villains. That is not how Olson wants to use history.

William Carlos Williams had done it that way. In "The Destruction of Tenochtitlan," a chapter of *In the American Grain*, Williams had taken sides, giving Montezuma "tact, self-control and remarkable grasp of the changing situation." "Montezuma has left no trace of cowardice upon the records," Williams writes (p. 34); "about the suave personality of this barbaric chieftain the liveliest, most airily expansive moods of the race did flower." Cortez, conversely, although "neither malicious, stupid nor blind," was "a conqueror like other conquerors" (p. 27). Olson had had his copy of the Boni first edition of *In the American Grain* (1925) since his Harvard days and admired its "vocative prose."[2] When he was first planning a book of his own on American history, he wrote in his notebook: "Consider Williams' *American Grain* for hints as to how to proceed."[3] But the evidence is that he subsequently repudiated Williams's approach, both its chronological order and its warmth.

What I think Olson is doing by means of Prescott's *History of the Conquest of Mexico* is arguing various points about change. He uses slivers of it here and there; in part 3, he is interested in tradition and violence. Those two words summarize this part of the poem in the outline found in the "Kingfishers" file at Storrs:

I	1	He & the birds Fernand	hangover change	
	2	Mao & the phenomenology of the birds	change, forward from what has rotted	The E on the stone
	3	Tradition, & violence	tradition & violence	stone

4 the feed-back,	brought back	Heraclitus
& person	to person	

Tradition and violence. Part 3 ends:

> And all now is war
> where so lately there was peace,
> and the sweet brotherhood, the use
> of tilled fields.
>
> (lines 90–94)

This is from the ending of Prescott's account of the Aztec priests (p. 194): "All was now confusion, tumult, and warlike menace, where so lately had been peace and the sweet brotherhood of nations." What Olson adds, the image of "tilled fields," helps to emphasize the traditional life broken by violence. The "treasures" of line 69 and following also reinforce the notion of tradition, but a tradition wrenched by the use to which the beautifully crafted ornaments were put—first by Montezuma in an attempt to buy off Cortez, and then by Cortez for a similar reason. The treasure was all sent to Spain as a gift in order to curry favor with the Court.

The E is a contrast, presumably tradition without violence:

> But the E
> cut so rudely on that oldest stone
> sounded otherwise,
> was differently heard.
>
> (lines 62–65)

As the poem stands, the contrast is with the conqueror of line 60. It is instructive in this instance, however, to go back to one of the worksheets in the "Kingfisher" file, where, after the line "he so resembles ourselves," we read:

> The note of the kingfisher is shrill. He is a solitary & pugnacious bird.
> But the E, cut so rudely on that oldest stone, sounded otherwise, and was differently heard. As, in another time, were treasures used.

Now we see a context in which the phrase "sounded otherwise" has an appropriate referent rather than hanging oddly as it does when the line about the kingfisher's shrill song is removed. For some reason, Olson wanted the kingfisher out, and we have to accept that. But this draft version does confirm that the kingfisher, in Olson's mind, is pretty unattractive. In fact, when it is dropped, the conquistador takes its place—the conquistador who began the dirtying of America from the very start.

II

We get no help from any draft of the poem in the respect to what remains a crux in interpretation:

> (and, later, much later, a fine ear thought
> a scarlet coat).
>
> (lines 67–68)

The parentheses indicate that this is very much an interpolation. We do not expect any help from the rest of the poem. We either know who the "fine ear" is or we do not. The poet says "much later," but how much later is that? Davenport (p. 255) found the phrase "scarlet bright" in Prescott. The line "Or scarlet bright, as in the wintry wood" is in Robert Southey's description of the Tlascalan army in his poem *Madoc*, as found in a footnote in the Modern Library edition (p. 235). But Olson did not mark the passage in his copy, nor is there evidence he ever considered Southey had a "fine ear." Besides, what could the Southey quote possibly mean, implanted in "The Kingfishers"? To propose it as a possibility means you do not really expect the poem to mean anything.

The actual phrase "scarlet coat" is found in a piece by Olson himself, a review of a book on Captain John Smith, the early explorer of the Atlantic seaboard of North America, the entrepreneur who has entered popular imagination with the story of his being saved from death by the Indian princess Pocahontas. The founding of the Jamestown colony in 1607 is sufficiently "later"; however, how does the "scarlet coat" fit the context? Here is the pertinent passage from Olson's review:

> they send a bird like Newport, as Captain of a ship, and with orders to dress Powhatan in a scarlet coat (that early, the English, were playing that game).[4]

"That game"? The "game" that was played all over the British Empire was to co-opt local chiefs by means of regalia. John Smith, with more than a modicum of honesty and common sense, disapproved of the attempt to bribe Powhatan with a scarlet coat. Now, this fits in with part 3 of "The Kingfishers" because Montezuma was trying to bribe Cortez with treasurers, and Cortez in his turn the Spanish Court.

But would Olson describe John Smith as "a fine ear"? Improbable as it may seem, that, I think, is precisely how Olson would describe him. "It's not true," he said in the review, "that Smith wasn't a great stylist." He speaks of "the very bite of his language" and gives several examples from Smith's prose. He included the whole of Smith's poem "The Sea Marke" in an early *Maximus* poem (I.69–70). Some college anthologies of American Literature have followed suit. It reads very well.

> Aloofe, aloofe; and come no neare,
>   the dangers doe appeare;
> Which if my ruine had not beene
>   you had not seene:
> I onely lie upon this shelfe
>   to be a marke to all
>   which on the same might fall,
> That none may perish but my selfe.

In view of Smith's fall from favor through no fault of his own, this image is quite moving. And it is not merely this one poem, but the fact that Smith could get his knowledge of the country into "prose like no one has since" that caused Olson from the platform at Berkeley to name him the first American writer, "that great successor to William Shakespeare" (*Muthologos* 1, p.142), and as a valediction at the end of his long reading to reiterate his belief that American writing was only just catching up with "the commonness of John Smith, who replaced, I believe directly, William Shakespeare" (*Muthologos* I, p. 156). It is an audacious notion—but one that Olson hazarded more than once in conversation (see *Guide*, p. 103)—that at Shakespeare's death in 1616 the spirit of the English Renaissance and its pride of language came across the Atlantic by means of the first American book, published that very year, John Smith's *Description of New England*. As Olson put it to Creeley in an unpublished letter of 14 April 1953, after typing out the whole of Smith's poem: "right out of W. Shax, Gent."

I don't know a better bet for the "scarlet coat" allusion. If John Smith as "the fine ear" is not correct, then we have a crossword clue still waiting to be deciphered. Can Olson expect his readers, even a persistent reader, to come up with a certain answer here? Perhaps he is content that there might be occasional blanks. Who says that there shall be no empty spaces in a poem? Cryptic allusiveness is bound to be sometimes an accidental concomitant to that energy spoken of in "Projective Verse," the natural movement of energy "instanter" from one perception to the next, to get said what has to be said without drag (*Selected Writings*, p. 17). The masters of twentieth-century poetry have surely established that obscurity is not to be taken as failure on the part of the poet but as a challenge to the reader. The work—if it gives one the sense that it is worth it—asks the reader to become educated in the way necessary to read it. It will survive with a few obscurities if its natural energies are right, and not curtailed for the sake of complete lucidity. I hope that Captain John Smith is the right answer here; however, lingering doubt is not necessarily harmful. It keeps the passage in one's mind. Obscurities do not push one away from a poem; they are places where one is motivated to keep reentering the poem, bringing subsequent reading and experience to bear.

III

Jumping to a further use of Prescott in "The Kingfishers" we have the following passage on Cortez destroying the Aztec temples:

> Fifty soldiers, at a signal from their general, sprang up the great stairway of the temple, entered the building on the summit, the walls of which were black with human gore, tore the huge wooden idols from their foundations, and dragged them to the edge of the terrace. (p. 195)

This becomes in part II:

> (of the two who first came, each a conquistador, one healed the other
> tore the eastern idols down, toppled

>   the temple walls, which, says the excuser
>   were black from human gore)
>
>   (lines 145–148)

—where the "excuser" is Bernal Diaz, whose *History of the Conquest*, written fifty years after the events in which he participated, is one of Prescott's chief sources. The loaded word "excuser" seems to imply that there is no excuse for Cortez's kind of desecration; yet at the same time, human sacrifice of thousands by Aztec priests is reliably attested to, and must be in the mind of both the poet and his reader.

Indeed, it is not only human sacrifice that the poet seems to want us to face up to at this point but also cannibalism. He quotes in Italian from Marco Polo's account of the Japanese he met enjoying human flesh, again a passage he marked in Prescott (a footnote to p. 698):

> Marco Polo notices a civilized people in South-eastern China, and another in Japan, who drank the blood and ate the flesh of their captives; esteeming it the most savory food in the world,—la più saporita et migliore, che si possa truovar al mondo. (Viaggi, lib. 2, cap. 75; lib. 3, 13, 14).

>   hear
>   hear, where the dry blood talks
>   where the old appetite walks
>
>   la piu saporita et migliore
>   che si possa truovar al mondo
>   (lines 149–153)

This gets us very deep into the springs of human nature, way beyond a poet-historian settling accounts with Cortez. Olson has pulled out of Prescott a sliver that hurts on a deep level of self-examination. We shall have to go into this dark side of things as subsequent sections of the poem take us there.

But we pull back for a moment to deal with something that might easily be passed over, but should not be: the one who "healed" (line 145). Cortez is not allowed to be a dramatic principal in the poem; this other conquistador is not developed at all beyond that mere reference. Yet at one point he was to have had pride of

4: Recurrences

place at the end of the poem. As Appendix E shows, Cabeza de Vaca was to have been introduced with the lines:

> in the juvescence came Cabeza not the least like a tiger
> and we will speak of him without gloss.

Parodying "Gerontion," this is another slap at T. S. Eliot, but it was dropped, and a formal invocation of Cabeza de Vaca was begun as the coda of the poem after "slain in the sun" (see Appendix F). The extant worksheets show two or three other tries at formulating a tribute; the temporarily finished lines are to be found in a letter of about 10 March 1949 in which Olson sends to Caresse Crosby his "day's work today," a part III of the poem, ending with the following lines:

> I invoke one man, he who was shipwrecked on this shore
> lost Europe's clothes, was naked how many winters,
> lived on shell-fish, was lacerated feet and skin, was slave,
> first trader, learned what tribes these were, walked,
> walked, found deer skin, clothed himself, walked
> as the doe walks, white man, white
> a second time
> a second time, and he only, of all, no one else, reborn!

A poet who can bring himself to cut out of a poem beautiful lines like these has a rare scrupulousness. What makes him go to such lengths to avoid the inspirational? Why can he not find a place in his poem for a good hero like Alvar Nunez Cabeza de Vaca?

The question becomes all the more puzzling when we trace how integral Cabeza always was in Olson's preliminary thinking about a book or a long poem on America. Butterick laid out a good many of these documents from the period 1946–48 in *OLSON* 5 (Spring 1976). Cabeza is everywhere:

> de Vaca   the image of all to follow (p. 12)

> Open here . . . CABEZA DE VACA: and turn back to Indians via de Vaca's medicine (p. 20)

> Cabeza may be you, the person you would choose to range the story of the WEST as he did first the LAND (p. 22)

> I propose to open with the extraordinary and little known story of CABEZA DE VACA, to "name" him, to cause us to place him in our experience, to fix him as predecessor, and thus to learn, by the addition of him, how to name ourselves (p. 27)
>
> The white line, major, of course, would start with Cabeza de Vaca, set Cortez off against him. (p. 32)

Cabeza de Vaca is interesting because of his misfortunes. He was forced to get to know the natives instead of conquering them. His journey by foot from the Atlantic coast to the Pacific would certainly have symbolic dimension for the poet who started his *Call Me Ishmael* with: "I take SPACE to be the central fact to man born in America" (p. 11). Cabeza had great potentiality for use, especially because Olson seems to have discovered him for himself—he is not in Prescott, he is not in *In the American Grain*.[5] Why was he dropped from "The Kingfishers" and not really used elsewhere?

In retrospect, Olson supposed that the issue was "blood." He is writing to Frances Boldereff in a letter of 14 July 1950 about Apollonius of Tyana's "antagonism to blood" as "a huge and present danger": this antagonism "must, like all Pythagoreanisms, be set aside, be watched, for its asceticism, its rubbing off, of the edge." Apollonius is, therefore, "to be taken as half—in fact as is my Cabeza. . . . I now see for the first time, why, in THE KS, I could not let him emerge any more than I did, why I had to add to him another . . . of the blood." Olson did not have a violent bone in his body, but the "blood" question seems to stay with him almost as an ancestral thing like Hawthorne's Salem witch trials. "What was slain in the sun" (line 187): something is there as an unresolved substratum. And apparently Cabeza is not the one to help him resolve it.

IV

The decision not to work through heroes, but to have the core of the poem be the problem of the self, was a long time coming. Actually, "The Kingfishers" goes back much further than we knew before Olson's copy of Prescott's *History of the Conquest of Mexico* surfaced; for under the signature on the flyleaf of that book is a date: "Spring 1941—towards the 'West.'" This early date is confirmed by the notebook "begun April 19th 1941," in which he lists Prescott among his books; and by a letter to Connie at that time in which he demonstrates how much he misses her by saying that he needs to drug himself to sleep at night by reading Prescott until his eyes are "too tired to stand more."[6] He also tells her he is going to write a poem from it: "what is going to be central is GOLD, perhaps as an image only, maybe as subject too, for the greed of the Spaniards for it and the Indians' confusion of the S as the breed of the Sun, the sons of white Quetzalcoatl, do join somehow, and ironically." On the basis of this evidence, one of the important items in *OLSON* 5, "An Outline of the Shape and the Characters of a Projected Poem called WEST," previously conjectured to be 1946, should now be dated 1941. Montezuma is one of the six figures structuring the poem-to-be, the others being Ulysses, Faust, Columbus, La Salle, and Balboa.[7] This would have been the youthful, ambitious "Poem of Western Man," with heroes as the measure of the American conscience. It was before he had found Cabeza, for he is not mentioned.

Olson got through the war years, got through *Call Me Ishmael*, and was ready to face the "West" project again. He wrote up a proposal and got a Viking contract for *Red, White and Black*.[8] He rewrote the proposal as a Guggenheim application and was awarded his second fellowship.[9] All should have been plain sailing for him to write a history book to cap all. He had certainly thought about it enough. But he waited and hesitated. Then on 6 April 1949 he wrote to his Viking editor, Monroe Engel, about a change of approach: "I have been trying myself out on a long poem." He sheepishly mentioned "the BOOK which we do not mention," and adds: "the long poem, I ought to tell you, has recurrencies which come off that same material." Here we have it, then. His reading of Prescott—"towards the 'West'"—long before in 1941, thought of as a long poem, then thought of as the prose book to follow *Call Me Ishmael*, and now rethought as the basis for "The Kingfishers": these are the recurrencies.

I am wondering if the genetic inscape of the final poem was not there from the start in "An Outline of the Shape and the Characters of a Projected Poem called WEST." The "Epilogue," according to the notes, envisioned a "figure, yet unnamed": "the man who, like Ulysses for the West, carries in him the seeds of the way of life which shall replace the West, and in a dying world is restless to open the new; confused, harried, but breathing the air of another Indies while those around him stifle from the dead will" (*OLSON* 5, p. 14). This figure breathes the air of an Indies that was Cortez's; he inherits the "spirit of place" that D. H. Lawrence identified as so tragically defined in America. The journey of the "healer" Cabeza de Vaca was a map of reparation up to a point. Now the figure stands facing the present. Let us give this unnamed figure its name: it is the self.

5
Self

I

Olson's outline of "The Kingfishers" (presented earlier) summarized part 4 in the following way:

| 4 | the feed-back & person | brought back to person | Heraclitus |

We are to be offered one of the most ancient definitions of "person" and one of the most recent:

> Not one death but many,
> not accumulation but change, the feed-back proves, the feed-back is the law
>   Into the same river no man steps twice
>   When fire dies air dies
>   No one remains, nor is, one.
>
>   (lines 94–99)

With the mention of feed-back, Norbert Wiener's *Cybernetics* is introduced; the rest is from Plutarch's "On the E at Delphi" again, where Heraclitus is quoted. Much of this section is drawn from a single small chapter of Plutarch's essay, which is best quoted in full for reference purposes:[1]

> XVIII. "For we ourselves have in reality no part in existence; for all mortal nature being in a state between birth and dissolution presents no more than an illusion, and a semblance, shapeless and unstable of itself, and if you will closely apply your thought, out of the wish to seize hold of the idea, just as the too strong grasping at water when

73

it is pressed together and condensed, loses it, for it slips through your fingers, in the same way Reason, in pursuing after the *appearances*, so extremely clear as they look, of each one of the conditions of life as they pass along, misses its aim; impinging on the one side against its coming into existence, on the other, against its going out; without ever laying hold upon it as a permanent thing, or as being in reality a power. It is not possible, according to Heraclitus, to step into the *same* river twice; neither is it to lay hold of mortal life twice, in the same condition; but by reason of the suddenness and speed of its mutation, it disperses and again brings together, or rather, neither *again* nor *afterwards*, but at one and the same time it subsists and it comes to an end; it approaches and it departs, wherefore it never ripens that of it which is born into actual being, by reason that Birth doth never cease nor stand still, but *transforms;* and out of the seed makes the embryo, then the child, then the youth, young man, full-grown man, elderly man, old man—obliterating the former growths and ages by those growing up over them. But we ridiculously fear *one* death, although we have already died, and are still dying, so many; for not only, as Heraclitus says, 'When fire dies is the birth of air, and when air dies is the birth of water,' but still more plainly may you see it from ourselves: the full-grown man perishes when the old man is produced, the youth had before perished into the full-grown man, and the child into the youth, and the infant into the child; and the 'yesterday' has died into the 'today,' and the 'today' is dying into the 'tomorrow,' and no one remains, nor is *one*, but we grow up many around one appearance and common model, whilst matter revolves around and slips away. Else how is it, if we remain the same, that we take pleasure in some things *now*, in different things *before;* we love contrary objects, we admire and find fault with them, we use other words, feel other passions; not having either appearance, figure, not disposition the same as before? To be in different states, without a change, is not a possible thing, and he that is *changed* is not the *same* person; but if he is not the same, he does not exist . . . this very thing (the change) he changes—growing one different person out of another; but Sense, through ignorance of reality, falsely pronounces that what appears *exists*."

Plutarch here is describing a world of appearances, of which we should have no fear, because it is mere appearance. For the neo-Platonist, reality lies in the eternal Being, which is true Existence. Olson does not follow Plutarch to this conclusion, nor does he accept any of the consolation that it is suggested meditation on the Eternal brings. He stays within Plutarch's mood, however,

5: Self

creating a threnody on the subject of mutability while ignoring the Idealism that might relieve it.

Change of life means that we have "not one death but many"[2]—the "deaths" being the crises and casualties in the war of living that make one older and wiser. This is not an uncommon metaphor. Olson would have seen it when he was reading Van Wyck Brooks's *The Life of Emerson* (1932) for his college paper on George Herbert's influence on Emerson: Herbert, "having lost the muse of his youth, found himself later, 'after so many deaths,' living and versing again" (p. 145). When he read it in Plutarch, it struck a chord. He took more from Plutarch in the same vein:

> Around an appearance, one common model, we grow up
> many. Else how is it,
> if we remain the same,
> we take pleasure now
> in what we did not take pleasure before? love
> contrary objects? admire and/or find fault? use
> other words, feel other passions, have
> nor figure, appearance, disposition, tissue
> the same?
> . . . .
>   between
> birth and the beginning of
> another fetid nest
>
> is change.
>
>   (lines 100–108, 120–23)

Reference to the quoted chapter XVIII will indicate where most of this comes from. The phrase "fetid nest" gives us a little bump, for we know where it comes from, and it is not Plutarch. But whatever its significance when it was previously used in line 49, its use here in summing up the span of a life serves to amplify the Plutarchian plangency of the whole passage. It is positively elegiac.

Is there something specific to account for the state of mourning that is detected here? We do not know what it was, but there was something. In a letter to Edward Dahlberg of 15 January 1949, just before "The Kingfishers" got started, Olson speaks of being "barren," stuck in "despair": "There is a quarrel in me, and I am unhinged. You must excuse me if I have nothing to say. I do not know which part of speech to speak from, what organ. Some certain things have left me. Others are not yet born. I gnaw, and gnaw. . . . I am merely slain by my own perplexities" (*Dahlberg Correspondence*, pp. 71–72). In a note to himself three days later he wrote: "I am obsessed today with how my love for my father has weakened my life" (Storrs's Miscellaneous file). His father had died fourteen years before; this is an ongoing mood. He may also have been anticipating in thought his mother's death which would occur a year later. The dark poem he included in the letter to Dahlberg would suggest this.[3]

Tanto e Amara

I have heard the dread song I had not heard
in the middle of life, I had not heard.
I was all eyes, all things were, now they are blind
and I am, I crawl, do not know where I go

You who have heard will understand
death is a remote beginning.
I am rudimentary.
I grow heart.

I stumbled when I saw, knew high passage, persons
one imperial nature whose conclusion was
nothing, it is nothing.
I know now it was nothing.

The wise man said, nothing dieth
but changing as they do one for another show
sundry formes. He lieth. I cannot have back my mother.

In the grave, before the dirt goes, will go my love.
And what shall I be, which forms will plague me then
where shall I go, in which ditch pour what blood to hear
her voice, the love I hear, that voice now mingled
in the song,
the song of the Worms?

Because he had been so attentive to life, the poet had not heard "the dread song" of death until now, when his father's "imperial nature" seems reduced to ignominy by the finality of death and when his mother's coming death is the imminent end of love. *Der Weg stirbt:* the path dies. This latter phrase, which Olson had found in Frobenius's *Paideuma*, was used for the first time in a poem called "Conqueror" of January 1948, which Olson revised a year later in the mood of "Tanto e Amara" to have it end with the lines: "it is better a worm gets us / in the end" (*Collected Poems*, pp. 72–73). The path dies. In this black mood the poet contradicts what the "wise man"—presumably Plutarch—once said: "nothing dieth / but changing as they do one for another show / sundry formes."[4] This was only a temporary depression, but it seems to be reflected in "The Kingfishers," undertaken soon afterwards, where part 4 lays out an ancient discussion of change, but without any of the traditional solace.

II

There are several times in Olson's life when we note he became sick when he was about to demand a great push of work from himself. This probably corresponds to the depression James Hillman calls "soul-making," a vale of tears essential to knowing oneself. "The Kingfishers" did get written, and it is in the end a positive poem. Olson borrows a lot of phrases from Plutarch, but he does come out at a different door. Because only God has an unchanging Being, says Plutarch, we mortals, because we change, cannot know ourselves. Olson does not go in this direction. For him, in the midst of change and loss, there is "this very thing you are":

>   is the birth of air, is
>   the birth of water, is
>   a state between
>   the origin and
>   the end, between
>   birth and the beginning of
>   another fetid nest
>
>   is change, presents
>   no more than itself

>   And the too strong grasping of it
>   when it is pressed together and condensed,
>   loses it
>
>   This very thing you are.
>   (lines 116–28)

What does not change is, at any point, the resistant presence of the individual and the will to be. After an important change or loss there comes the "recognition" that is spoken of as the moment of tragedy. One looks in the mirror and says, "What have I become now?" And the mirror answers back: "This very thing you are."

This is instinctual knowledge, and I take these lines to be pushing open the door not into God's universe but the "human universe" and its laws. With the phrase "too strong grasping of it" Olson has slipped Plutarch's words out from neo-Platonic thought, so that they no longer register our failure to grasp Ideal entities but our failure to turn to intuitive knowledge of the self. Olson has had the growing feeling that it has been "logic and classification" as habits of thought, from Aristotle on down, which "hugely intermit our participation in our experience"[5] (i.e., the too strong grasping after fact and reason prevent us from knowing ourselves instinctually). Though Olson's argument leads into the world not out of it, he shares Plutarch's antipathy to Reason:

> analysis only accomplishes a *description*, does not come to grips with what really matters: that a thing, any thing, impinges on us by a more important fact, its self-existence, without reference to any other thing, in short, the very character of it which calls our attention to it, which wants us to know more about it, its particularity. This is what we are confronted by, not the thing's "class," any hierarchy, of quality or quantity, but the thing itself.

Here in the "Human Universe" essay, written in June 1951 (*Selected Writings*, p. 56), Olson is distilling much of his thinking since "The Kingfishers" started him hunting among these stones. Because "man is himself an object,"[6] then, you present yourself to yourself not in terms of any class or hierarchy but in terms of your own "self-existence," as the very thing you are.

One could quote at length from "Human Universe" to see what Olson came to consider the laws of "what goes on each split second"

(*Selected Writings*, p. 56); however, the poet of "The Kingfishers" has not got as far as he would get in the Yucatan two years later. How far had he got? I cite an interesting letter dated 13 January 1949 that Olson drafted to Natasha Goldowski of Black Mountain College, and probably did not send, for it exists in an unfinished form in the Olson Archive at Storrs. The first basic principle lying behind the phrase "this very thing you are" is the physiological basis for human existence. The extract that follows has as its starting point the same concern as that found in the poem "La Préface." What makes that poem a preface to all that follows is the terrible knowledge of what happened in the Nazi extermination camps. The most crucial influence Corrado Cagli had on Olson was his bringing back from liberated Europe drawings he made when he accompanied Allied army units as they opened up Buchenwald. Olson wrote "La Préface" about May 1946 for an exhibition in Chicago of these drawings "from that ultimate experience" (note at Storrs). Perhaps because of the personal way in which this message was brought to his consciousness, Olson was affected very deeply. But how do you write about it?

> You, do not you speak who know not.
>
> > "I will die about April 1st . . ." going off
> > "I weigh, I think, 80 lbs . . ." scratch
> > "My name is NO RACE" address
> > Buchenwald new Altamira cave
> > > (*Selected Writings*, p. 160)

"La Préface" is a reaction in a fragmented form. It implies in its very title that more is needed. A month or so before "The Kingfishers" was taking shape, Olson wrote to Natasha Goldowski:

> when a number of men reduce man as value to so much soap, superphosphate for soil, fillings and shoes for sale, to oppose them other men have only one point of resistance to such fragmentation, one organized ground, a ground they come to by a way the precise contrary of the cross, of spirit, in the old sense, in old mouths.

(Olson is not led to religion by the knowledge of inhuman terror.)

> It is a man's own physiology he is forced to arrive at, and he arrives at it by the way of the beast, by the way of man and the Beast. . . .

> It is his body that is man's answer, his body intact and fought for, the absolute of his organism in its simplest terms, this structure evolved by mutations of nature
>> "nothing dieth, but in changing as they
>> doe one for another they show sundry formes"
> repeated in each act of birth, the animal man, the house he is, the house that moves, breathes, acts, the house where his life is, where he lives against the enemy, this citadel where he is based now more certainly than ever—besieged, overthrown—its power his only power (bone muscle nerve blood brain) its fragile mortal force its oldest eternity, nature's: RESISTANCE.

When this letter (in the Olson archive at Storrs) takes its final form as the essay "The Resistance," Olson adds a repudiation of what he calls "the fraud": "This organism now our citadel never was cathedral, draughty tenement of soul" (*Selected Writings*, pp. 13–14).[7] It is the primacy of physicality—not spirituality—that is established in Olson's thinking before "The Kingfishers." Then later, in "Human Universe," we get such statements as, "If there is any absolute, it is never more than this one, you, this instant, in action" (*Selected Writings*, p. 55). Olson is establishing a basically humanist moral structure from the power of unaccommodated man. This means that we can put great weight on line 128 "This very thing you are" as rallying strongly against the bewilderment of such lines as line 99 "No one remains, nor is, one."

We have seen an Olson strengthened by facing the fact of the holocaust as though he were a survivor having only his body with which to resist it. From this he intuits a philosophy of physicality, which gets him to the other side of despair. I am not saying that Buchenwald is in "The Kingfishers"; but the strength from having written "La Préface" is there. He is not going to accept the role that Plutarch gives humankind, that of the victim of mutability. He goes along with Plutarch and his own sadness for a while, and then stiffens the stem of the poem with "This very thing you are." There is not much pessimism in Olson's published works. The downers "Tanto e Amara" and "Conqueror" were not sent out for publication. "The Kingfishers" was; it raises itself up.

III

Immediately he heard about Cybernetics, Olson had the idea that it might have a bearing on the question of change within continuity. In the same letter of 13 January 1949 quoted earlier, Olson is asking Natasha Goldowski about something they discussed on his most recent visit to Black Mountain: "I want you again to tell me the name of that science of measure which is the 'latest thing,' please." When he excuses himself by saying, "I have no mind to retain polysyllables," we can be sure he is trying to remember the word "cybernetics," heard in conversation or at the reading Goldowski gave from Norbert Wiener's book *Cybernetics* (New York: John Wiley, 1948) in proofsheets.[8] Mary Emma Harris in *The Arts at Black Mountain College* has described Goldowski as "an exuberant woman," who "not only insisted on a high level of intellectual discipline from her students, but also entered enthusiastically into college life." She was at this out-of-the-way college only because, "after the war, she, like others with relatives behind the Iron Curtain, lost her clearance to work on government research projects."[9] This was the kind of person Olson began to know when he started his visits to BMC in 1948. The *Scientific American*, his favorite newsstand reading later, had not yet come into existence in its present form. He got the latest news from people like Natasha Goldowski. He put the news straight into a poem.

> We can be precise. The factors are
> in the animal and/or the machine the factors are
> communication and/or control, both involve
> the message. And what is the message? The message is
> a discrete or continuous sequence of measurable events distributed
>   in time.
>
> (lines 111–13)

Olson is using the full title of the book, *Cybernetics or Control and Communication in the Animal and the Machine,* and also the introduction (p. 8): "The message is a discrete or continuous sequence of measurable events distributed in time."

That "we can be precise" is exactly what Plutarch was saying was not possible. Olson intuited the value of the concept of "feed-back" (pp. 6–8 of Wiener's introduction) as a better way of understanding precisely how change and continuity work: "the feed-back proves, the feed-back is the law" (lines 95–96). "Feed-back" is the name given to the manner in which a system, the human body, say, guides its action by means of a servomechanism that notices error, corrects it, and makes sure the system stays on a predetermined course of action. With feed-back *der weg* should not *stirbt*. For Olson it became a matter of the eyes, the fingertips, and the tissue of the body. ("Tissue," by the way, was something added to Plutarch's list in line 107: "figure, appearance, disposition, tissue.") Eyes and fingertips are important in the "Human Universe" essay. Tissue, or the visceral, leads forward to the "Proprioception" essay of 1959—though presumably Olson first came across the word "proprioceptive" in the introduction to *Cybernetics* (p. 7), and then later turned to his Webster's Collegiate Dictionary for the definition he gave in the essay: "sensibility within the organism by movement of its own tissues."[10] Proprioception is essentially a feed-back process, very precise in its autonomic mode. These are the unerring internal rhythms: "a discrete or continuous sequence of measurable events distributed in time." Proprioception is "Know thyself" on an instinctive physical level.

As Davenport pointed out (p. 256), the words "discrete" and "continuous" are later found in connection with the mathematician Riemann in the essay "Equal, That Is, to the Real Itself." Olson turned to mathematics, to the extent that he was capable of, for its sense of "how we know and present the real."[11] But this is later, after he has read many *Scientific Americans*. For "The Kingfishers" he has only the latest "latest thing," cybernetics, as an introduction to the mathematical notation of the metrical field.

IV

This use of cybernetics is probably as much science as the poem could take. It is, anyway, unexpected in a poem to find such technical words as "feed-back" and "message." Their shock value even in small doses bolsters the argument for knowable reality as against Plutarch's scorn of appearances. If there is not more there than meets the eye, there is certainly not less.

There is a worksheet in the "Kingfishers" file at Storrs that shows Olson trying to apply further physics to a definition of the self and change. Though he dropped the attempt, it is nevertheless interesting as part of the thinking behind his "Proteid." Here is the poem as derived from the worked draft (see Appendix B):

5: Self

What you are / all is

a certain quantum, arrived at by accumulation,
which quantum, by that accumulation, becomes
what all is, what you are, that which may
change
change, which better be understood to be
energy, given off

light, which is now proved to be
both particle and wave

what you are, what all is
uncertain. . . . yet, uncertain
only in respect to when,
in what direction, where
you shall express yourself, burst

la lumiere,
la lumiere et la matiere
is one

is energy in and out, is
constant, is inconstant
in respect solely to
choice, to the moment of
change, to the giving off of
light

It is necessary now to put it this way:
the discontinuous is
the law, uncertainty is
the principle, nature
makes nothing but
jumps

We know now,
let Leibnitz holler, and go,
we know now how we must act,
we know
what the eye is, how
he who rules us
converts, what it is
we must do

> let one constant, "h," be added,
> to the five, to the E, let h be added,
> to light and to matter
> let the h be added, even though,
> to this day, it is susceptible of
> no interpretation
>
> let you be added,
> let you be that constant,
> let you observe
> in nature's sentence
> that one undefinable syllable,
> let you be
>
> CHANGE

Olson's specific source for this poem is not at present known. With the atom bomb, subatomic quantum physics was having much exposure—though Planck's constant h goes back to the first decade of the century. Olson seems to be punning on the Delphic E and the equation for quantum energy, $E = h\nu$, to bring things up to date. He thought better, in the end, of using quantum theory. The uncertainty principle defies common sense and does not, in any case, mean uncertainty, except in limited subatomic situations, if there. Olson is far more interested in the h constant, which is a known thing. We too can know ourselves and be constant. The essence of the poem is the glorious self-sufficiency of the human being.

6
Pejorocracy

I

Part II of "The Kingfishers" contrasts East and West, and begins with three strong chords of various harmonics that, when researched, are seen to be announcing the theme. Olson wrote in pencil "Asia and Aztecs compared" above the title of William Prescott's appendix "Origin of Mexican Civilization." If American aboriginal civilization had its origins in Asia, that fact provides a fixed point for looking again to the Far East.

> They buried their dead in a sitting posture
> serpent   cane   razor   ray of the sun.
>   (lines 129–30)

"Who can doubt the existence of an affinity, or, at least, intercourse, between tribes, who had the same strange habit of burying the dead in a sitting posture"—in this opinion concerning Asian and American first peoples, Prescott (p. 699) is relying on anthropological data of the time. The list in the second line above is easily seen to come from Prescott's footnote (p. 700): "The lunar calendar of the Hindoos exhibits a correspondence equally extraordinary. Seven of the terms agree with those of the Aztecs, namely, serpent, cane, razor, path of the sun, dog's tail, house." This passage is marked by Olson in his copy.

The word "Cioacoatl" is circled (p. 696), with Olson's marginal note, "Baptism." He underlines in the footnote the words, "with her face towards the west." Prescott's playing on Christian and Pagan similarities adds to the East-West theme and gives Olson his lines 131–33:

> And she sprinkled water on the head of the child, crying
> "Cioa-coatl! Cioa-coatl!"
> with her face to the west.

The information in the next lines is not from Prescott, nor likely from any printed source. Olson is, I believe, remembering Professor Frederick Merk's lectures in "History 62 The Westward Movement" at Harvard in 1937–38. When citing the evidence for South American Indians coming from the Mongoloid branch, Merk included "similarities in parasites that prey upon them—Mongolian louse on pre-1492 Peru mummies."[1] It is a striking enough detail to remain in the memory:

> Where the bones are found, in each personal heap
> with what each enjoyed, there is always
> the Mongolian louse.
>
> (lines 134–36)

These three groups of images at the beginning of part II announcing the East-West theme are the nearest thing to a static ideogram in the poem. I prefer to think of them as similar to the intricately pointed, thematically pictorial capital letters that begin sections of an illuminated medieval manuscript.

With lines 137–38, the theme is made explicit: "The light is in the east. Yes. And we must rise, act. Yet / in the west. . . ." Mao's words of part 2 are here translated and are about to be applied to us of the west, where "despite the apparent darkness," we may begin to find our way again, if we look long enough for it.

II

The West has its own particular problem: hypocrisy, symbolized in the whiteness of the skin that covers a multitude of sins. "I'm the White Man," Olson announced from the platform at Berkeley, with more than a touch of ironic heaviness. "That famous thing, the White Man, the ultimate paleface, the noncorruptible, the Good, the thing that runs this country, or that *is* this country" (*Muthologos* 1, p. 133). His tone was an acknowledgement that European Americans are stuck with that inescapable "lily white" mask, "the whiteness / which covers all" of lines 138–39. His mentor Herman Melville had already untagged the inherited moral labels from the words "white" and "black" in chapter XLII of *Moby-Dick*, "The Whiteness of the Whale," where whiteness is discussed as an ambiguous if not an outright deceptive quality. "It was the whiteness of the whale," says Ishmael in that chapter, "that above all things apalled me." This is a "palsied universe" and "the wretched infidel gazes himself blind at the monumental white shroud that wraps all the prospect around him." In April 1948, taking up the challenge to make a dance-play based on Ahab's "fiery hunt," Olson recast these lines on the menacing whiteness as follows:

> What whiteness is this that the night has left? . . .
> Such light is holy in another place. . . .
> But on this sea, in this blank morning of our year,
> with this wild leader in his wild pursuit,
> this color without color locks us in
> a palsy, new-found fear.
> This white that stares me in the face
> looks at me like a dusted enemy.[2]

Merton Sealts, the Melville scholar, tells of meeting Olson for the first time and showing him an article he had just written. Olson read it and looked up, saying, "Well, I see that the White Death has descended upon *you* too!"[3] This was early 1941; their relationship as scholars—with persistence—developed into one of trust. It is such persistence being asked of us in part II of "The Kingfishers" (lines 139, 142):

> . . . if you look, if you can bear, if you can, long enough
> so you must, and, in that whiteness, into that face, with what
> candor, look.

The whited sepulcher of Western civilization must be examined at great length. How persistent must one be? How long is enough?

The answer is given in a rather strange comparison, interpolated at lines 140–41 in the poem:

> as long as it was necessary for him, my guide
> to look into the yellow of that longest-lasting rose

—that is, as long as it took Dante, having gone through all the darknesses of hell and all the grays of purgatory, to take in the pure light when he arrived at the heavenly throne, which, as described in *Paradiso* canto xxx, has the appearance from a distance of a yellow, eternal rose.[4] Davenport (p. 257) feels that Olson's guide would be Ezra Pound. He acknowledges that the rose image is from Dante, but he also believes that Olson was thinking of the "model civilization" that Pound offered in the *Pisan Cantos*. Olson brought this on himself by using the word "candor," which Pound took out a sort of copyright on by his use of it in the *Pisan Cantos*. But I think Pound as an intermediary is simply superfluous here. Someone brought up to attend mass weekly by a strict Roman Catholic mother (at least until he left home for college) might claim his own access to Dante.

On 11 May 1948 Olson wrote to Frances Boldereff: "Back on Dante yesterday"; and on the same day wrote to Viking for their *Portable Dante*.[5] It was not *The Divine Comedy* he was after but the *De Vulgare Eloquentia*. Soon after, he was writing in "More Notes Toward the Proposition: Man is Prospective" (published posthumously in *boundary 2*) that Dante's account of the revolution in language in his own time in *De Vulgare Eloquentia* "is of such profundity that it behooves any of us to know and apply it to present needs" (p. 5). Dante is none other than the guide who led Olson to undertake an *ars poetica* for the midtwentieth century, the essay "Projective Verse." Dante was also a guide in respect to the methodology of a long poem: that it should include the author—"the which is Dante's method."[6] When he was later undertaking the *Maximus Poems*, Olson (Robin Blaser tells me) spoke constantly of Dante in conversation; but already with "The Kingfishers" we have a poem where, with part III, the author enters the poem.

An interesting point is that Dante in *Paradiso* has to look through appearances to the essence, as though it had previously been masked.

> Then—as folk under masks seem other than before,
> if they do off the semblance not their own wherein they hid them,—
>
> so changed before me into ampler joyance the flowers and
> the sparks, that I saw both the two courts of heaven manifested.[7]

6: Pejorocracy

One recalls the famous "pasteboard mask" speech of Ahab's in chapter XXXVI of *Moby-Dick*, a diabolical mirroring of Dante's in the passage above. Dante is permitted, but Ahab is willing to strike through the mask at God if that's what it takes to get at the truth of the real. There seems to be something equally at stake in Olson's demand that we look long

> where it hides, look
> in the eye how it runs
> in the flesh / chalk.
>
> (lines 154–56)

Behind the sanctimoniousness of our history books and the self-satisfied opulence of our society lies hidden—what?

The clue is given by the Marco Polo quotation about the eating of human flesh (lines 149–53), which we have already touched on and now see fits into the theme of cannibalism, a theme which has absorbed and disturbed Olson since he read about the Donner party and tied it in with Melville. For "the old appetite" is the "First Fact" of *Call Me Ishmael* (the Owen Chase narrative). Olson was given a sense of the cannibalism of the sea from Melville and found such things lurking in the depths of *Moby-Dick* that he had to apply Freud's *Moses and Monotheism* to bear on it, in his chapter "The book of the law of the blood": "It is cannibalism. Even Ishmael, the orphan who survives the destruction, cries out: 'I myself am a savage, owing no allegiance but to the King of Cannibals'" (p. 81). If we look deep enough, long enough, any of us might be; all of us are.

Nearer to the time of "The Kingfishers," we have the evidence of a letter to Frank Moore of 12 May 1949, in which Olson, responding to the subject of cannibalism in the *Odyssey* raised by Moore, asks provocatively: "Is it (cannibalism) not more than a dromenon the race puts behind it in passage civilizationwards? is it not, and does it not remain, despite all euphemisms (bulls, eucharist, war) the ROOT ACT?"—adding a psychological comment: "consider the craving of nakedness, exposure, teeth, rending (which rending, not done, creates stoppages now called several other misleading names)." In August 1949 Olson directed students in a theater exercise based on the Cyclops episode in the *Odyssey*. One does not hear of any teeth rending, but one wonders. In any case, on this evidence, we can say that Olson was not pulling any punches in part II of "The Kingfishers": behind the mask of white civilization is the "root act" of cannibalism. This, the worst that human beings can do to each other, is implicit in all other crimes of whatever order of inhumanity and, therefore, all-pervasive in what the poet here calls "pejorocracy."

III

"Pejorocracy" means literally "worse rule." It comes into the poem with line 167: "what pudor pejorocracy affronts"—where Olson is saying that pudor (modesty, decorum) is affronted by the worsening state of things in our time. It was a word newly made available by Pound; it appears in canto 79 of *The Pisan Cantos*. To the extent that he was willing to steal this word, Olson felt he shared Pound's exasperation at the political situation. Olson used it again a year later in the first *Maximus:* "pejorocracy is here, now / that street-cars . . . twitter" (I.3). This refers to the music that was being piped into public transportation at that time. Olson called it "mu-sick" later in the poem and repeated his complaint in one of "The Songs of Maximus":

> But that the car doesn't, that no moving thing moves
> without that song I'd void my ear of, the musickracket
> of all ownership. (I.14)

Olson here expands the offense to the affront that ownership cannot help but offer to the dispossessed (Olson had trouble with his own absentee landlady). This is a far cry from Buchenwald. It is a postwar world where pejorocracy is torts, not torture:

> with what violence benevolence is bought
> what cost in gesture justice brings
> what wrongs domestic rights involve
> what stalks
> this silence.
>
> (lines 162–66)

Indeed, if we take seriously the words "benevolence," "justice," and "rights" in this passage, there is no evil intent involved, as such. It is just that these abstract ideals seem to produce adverse effects when put into practice. For instance, we assume from "Song 5" of "The Songs of Maximus" that Olson thinks an agency like the United Nations Food and Agricultural Organization is likely to do more harm than good:

> I have seen faces of want,
> and have not wanted the FAO.
>
> (I.16)

Because the FAO is a very new organization at this time, this opinion is sheer prejudice. Yes, Olson is prejudiced; he has an inbuilt assumption that Yankee self-reliance will be the better way. John Chapman was from Boston; he got the idea of supplying orchards to the new frontier settlements. The myth of Johnny Appleseed grew up around him; he also made quite a lot of money. Against FAO, Olson puts: "Appleseed / . . . any of us / New England" (I. 16).

Emerson's essay "Self-Reliance" may be behind this. Olson simply cannot stand state charity. There are lines in "Song 3" that can be understood in terms of this antipathy (which otherwise would cause consternation):

> In the face of sweetness,
> piss
> In the time of goodness,
> go side, go
> smashing, beat them.
>
> (I. 14)

One thinks of some saccharine social worker taking a child away from its mother, then the "piss" sounds right.[8] With what violence benevolence is bought! What stalks the silence is a mephistopheles asking you to sell your soul to the system, to surrender your independence for dubious rights. The secret of Olson's resistance to this particular devil was that he could do with very little in the way of material possessions. He sings his defiance in *The Maximus Poems:*

> In the midst of plenty, walk
> as close to

>   bare
>   . . .
>   In the land of plenty, have
>   nothing to do with it
>   take the way of
>   the lowest.
>
>   (I. 14–15)

Olson had the advantage of being born poor. He was poor all his life, except that, when he had a windfall, he spent it, like his father did, on treats all round. "The Songs of Maximus" receives a gloss from a letter to Robert Creeley of 25 October 1950:

> Funny, the way I like the odds against: even the plumbing. Don't fix. Figure, play it the way it comes out. Protest, I suppose. Work with how it comes, don't fix—or rather DON'T BUY. . . . DON'T BUY— what they've got to offer. . . . Keep dough for wine. Food. Movement. Beat em. Beat em by not needing them. The WAY.[9]

Later, in *Mayan Letters*, Olson expresses kinship with the poverty of Mexico, and the way it is worn (*Selected Writings*, p. 93): "I come on, here, what seems to me the real, live clue to the results of what I keep gabbing about, *another* humanism. For it is so much a matter of resistance." Something of the survival ethos of *l'univers concentrationaire*[10] continues into ordinary life, and, in this less dire setting, nurtures positive values.

It is not inappropriate, therefore, for Olson to think of the one great tragedy of consumerism, Shakespeare's *Timon of Athens*, and borrow phrases from it for the first of the following lines (168–71) of "The Kingfishers":

>   how awe, night-rest and neighborhood can rot
>   what breeds where dirtiness is law
>   what crawls
>   below

Here are the money maggots undermining the health of the polis, as Timon saw them after he had lost his credit card.[11]

And there does not seem to be too much hope for us in the poem so far, unless one knows the importance of the one who "healed," unless one listens to Mao's "rise, act," or unless one senses a happier prognosis in lines 157–60:

6: Pejorocracy

>   but under these petals
>   in the emptiness
>   regard the light, contemplate
>   the flower

Are we to connect this flower back to the "longest lasting rose" of Dante's Paradise? It makes me uneasy to think of doing so. Appendix C shows that "whence it arose" takes us inside the skull to the god at the crossroads of the brain. This "god" does make an answer, but Olson does not allow us to know this until the poem "The Praises" (lines 91 and following). With "The Kingfishers" we are stuck with "what crawls below," and I don't think we are allowed more than that. We have here what used to be called "A General Satire of the World." There seems, at this point, to be no alleviation. In the worksheet Appendix D, there was to have been a question:

>   can you find
>   light
>   shall the east uncover
>   enable you to recover
>   the light[?]

These lines were left out of the finished poem, perhaps because the question is too blatant, and the answer—given the pejorocracy that covers all—too easily a "no."

7
The Advantage

I

On 27 May 1948 Olson asked himself: "Is it possible to do a long poem called WEST?"—that is, without "a strong injection of the poet's self." Whitman and Pound manage to be actors in the scene of their own poems; so does Dante. "By contrast Homer and Shakespeare keep themselves out" (*OLSON* 5, p. 38). Up to the end of part II of "The Kingfishers" Olson has mostly kept himself out. At a certain point in the worksheets of the umbrella poem "Proteid" at Storrs, wondering out loud about how to finish the poem, he knew it would be with "neither a bird nor a god":

> human personality is the only path and instrument which is of any interest in the pursuit of reality and is, therefore, the only extension beyond reality. Keep dragging the parts of this verse back to man and his power, setting that ordinary magic against all earlier forms.

This same draft page indicates that what Olson had in mind was to bring the various lines of the poem together in the figure of Quetzalcoatl:

> Neither a bird nor a god, it turns out,
> but that simplest of things, an extraordinary man,
> who died, or was immolated, April 5, 1208, who, in his life,
> did certain things which had value for
> others.

The extensive working and reworking of the Quetzalcoatl material shows how hard Olson tried to keep himself out.[1] But "Know thyself!" does not mean "Know Quetzalcoatl!" The exhortation carved at Delphi is the sure answer to all petitioners: If you know yourself, you will know what to do about any problem; you will know how to be of use to yourself and others. And you can enter your poem.

"Know thyself!" It is on the basis of an amplitude of experience, registered in one's psyche, that one can present oneself objectively as the subject of a poem. In a Storrs manuscript (not in the "Kingfishers" file but seeming as though it ought to be), Olson writes a "CREDO." The "necessities" are that one should be (1) a phenomenologist, "viz, to get it down as it is, with the avoidance of (avert, avert) all interpretation, explanation, evaluation"; (2) an objectivist, "to render all abstractions by way of object"; and (3) oogenetic, which means "formation of the egg and its preparation for fertilization and development." This third function "allows for the recurrence of the subjective when it has been earned." "The Kingfishers" up to part II has shown Olson as phenomenologist and objectivist. Now he is ready to enter the poem in his own person; the subjective has been earned.

By early 1949 the poet, having made the decision to be in the poem, has included in a letter to Caresse Crosby what is recognizably close to the present part III of "The Kingfishers" (letter at Southern Illinois):

> I am no Greek,
> hath not th'advantage.
> And of course no Roman:
> who can take no risk that matters,
> the risk of beauty least of all.
> Thus, and only thus, no tragedy.
>
> But I have my kin. Despite the disadvantage,
> it works out this way. I have an epigraph. I quote:
> si j'ai du goût, ce n'est guères
> que pour la terre et les pierres.
> In other words, on this continent,
> what was slain in the sun.

These lines take us a good way toward the published part III: the poet is sorting out with whom he feels kinship and with whom he does not. The quotation in French is the same as the final version. It is from Rimbaud's "Un Saison en enfer," and can be translated: "If I have any appetite, it is for little else but earth and stones."

This is, in graphic form, a rock-bottom position from which to make a start. Olson acknowledges one notable predecessor, Arthur Rimbaud.

II

Olson did not become acquainted with Rimbaud until he began reading Enid Starkie's biography *Arthur Rimbaud* (1938 ed.) in 1945. A "Key West II" notebook entry for 16 February is headed, "Rimbaud's life (I do not know his poetry)":

> I cannot think of another man as SERIOUS as Arthur Rimbaud, faulty with seriousness. The overwhelming STRENGTH of the man. I have no image of the pretty boy, the Boheme. But the image of a rough, sure, hard like platinum is. The summer of Saison d'enfer is the huge and lovely climax.

He sketches out a play on Rimbaud's life. On 20–24 February 1945 he writes a long biographical poem called "The True Life of Arthur Rimbaud," which is preserved as a nine-page typescript at Storrs. On 26 February he puts in the notebook a significant quotation from Rimbaud; "the first aim of the poet must be to know himself fully." With this quotation he has already picked out an aspect of the young Rimbaud that will fit into the "Know thyself" theme of "The Kingfishers." As he put it in another poem about this time, Rimbaud was "as red-hot an arrow as a man can be":

> knew so much because that arrow
> in repulse cross and criss-crossed
> one core of such reality
> he burned it clear, without
> destroying it.
>
> Not by impulse but by repulse
> he totally pierced
> childhood.[2]

This is the self-knowledge that caused Rimbaud to drop poetry and become a merchant in Africa. Even before "The Kingfishers" Olson had probably run into the striking quotation from Wallace

Fowlie's book *Rimbaud* (1946): "Rimbaud moved on to the despair which lies beyond sin and then sought what lies beyond despair."³ Olson paraphrased it several times as a question: "What's on the other side of despair?"⁴ Giving Rimbaud credit for having found out, Olson summed it up by stating that Rimbaud "had been so fierce as to come to totality, the condition of the Hero" (*Human Universe*, p. 116). It is as a hero, then, not a literary figure, that Rimbaud enters "The Kingfishers"; and in the final version of these lines is granted what Olson himself does not have: Courage.

> It works out this way, despite the disadvantage.
> I offer, in explanation, a quote:
> si j'ai du goût, ce n'est guères
> que pour la terre et les pierres
>
> Despite the discrepancy (an ocean   courage   age)
> this is also true: if I have any taste
> it is only because I have interested myself
> in what was slain in the sun.
>
> (lines 180–187)

He is separated from Rimbaud by age difference, the differing milieu of Europe, and by his comparative lack of courage to make decisions. Rimbuad would not have hesitated to go fight in the Spanish Civil War, would he? Olson could not make his mind up to go. Rimbaud had the will to change his life, not once but twice. Olson felt he had been pushed by circumstances into his life moves. Olson envied Rimbaud's ability to go back to ground, and he felt kinship with him in that regard. The quotation about "la terre et les pierres" has probably no more significance than that; nor was "what was slain in the sun" meant to be quite so melodramatic as it sounds. We should not narrow it down to Aztec human sacrifice, though that could be included in its vagueness, which seems to potentially embrace wide concerns in psychology and archeology.

We must not sell Olson short, even though he seems himself to want to do in comparison with Rimbaud. This is the moment of the dawning of the postmodern, as he was later able to formulate it:

> This is the morning, after the dispersion, and the work of the morning is methodology: how to use oneself, and on what. That is my profession. I am an archeologist of morning.⁵

In this context, Olson considered Rimbaud one of the four, along with Melville, Dostoevsky, and Lawrence, who created the possibility of the new: "They put men forward into the post-modern."[6] He did not write an essay on Rimbaud, as he did on Dostoevsky, Lawrence, and Melville; therefore, we are not exactly sure how and why Rimbaud gained the status of kin. There is a letter of 15 March 1951 to Creeley devoted in large part to Rimbaud, where Olson says he does not "know" Rimbaud but still takes him as "kin": "I come back to an old feeling, that Rimbaud saw there was nothing more to be done, *then*, that, still, he outranks us *now*, that, not one of us has matched now, what he is capable of, granting him the century sleep I think he took—with his eyes, open" (*Creeley Correspondence* 5, pp. 76–77). In some way, Rimbaud defines the previous epoch and the next.

At the same time, despite any envy there may have been, Olson knows that he has to live in his own world, and it is not like Rimbaud's. As he put it in the same letter to Creeley: "I do not take it as yours, or mine, or Gerhardt's requirement, that, we rustle crusts in Paris ashcans. Or pick up a poisoned leg, and lose it, anywhere" (p. 77). Transferred to present-day America, where would realistic reevaluations take a person of Olson's ability? At the end of our poem, he is still searching for the answer "among stones." The image hints that the way will be discovered in a paradox: that the move to the future is by attention to the archaic past, that the morning requires archeology.

Olson expressed this paradox of post-modernism (the concept, it should be stressed, as Olson defined it, not as it has been variously defined ad nauseam by myriad critics) in one of the "Kingfisher" worksheets:

> in this thickness
> from what paradox act leaps out
> what honey is where maggots are

—which becomes in the final poem lines 188–89:

> I pose you your question:
> shall you uncover honey / where maggots are?

Olson is drawing here on a proverbial expression in the Bible (Judg. 14:5–9), where Samson kills a lion and, coming back later, sees "a swarm of bees in the body of the lion, and honey." In other words, bees can make use of the rotting carcass of a lion; can you make use of the apparently dead past, Western civilization? The answer will be not a firm yes; for one makes use of Western civilization now by leapfrogging over it backward in history, to Sumer, for example, or by going outside of it to present-day remains of the primitive, the Maya, say, as Olson did, unable to get enough money to go to the eastern Mediterranean. "Sumeria (and the Maya)," Olson wrote to Creeley in August 1951, "teaches us abt civilization—in other words, are the sources, now, of what is actually culture—that after the ICE, there was CITY—and with CITY man as interesting creature began, in the same sense that he remains interesting now—as daily life character" *(Creeley Correspondence* 7, p. 70). How shall I conduct myself, the poet is asking, as a "daily life character"? If the poem ends with that question, it is likely that the poem itself, the road by which the question came to be asked, will give hints of "a preparatory state which is the condition of conviction" (*Muthologos* 1, p. 109). Yes, we might make honey eventually; we might have a home in the universe. As a matter of fact, the poem does not end with a question but a statement: "I hunt among stones." The conviction is gathering some force.

III

In contrast to a beginning of minute specificity, the ending of "The Kingfishers" tends toward broad implications. For his final thought, Olson uses an analogy (honey from a corpse) instead of a delineated problem; the hunting among stones is vague (what stones?). I find myself almost wishing Davenport was right in seeing a reference here to a particular source, the opening lines of *The Pisan Cantos* ("That maggots shd/ eat the dead bullock"). The question then would be specific enough, addressed to Pound: Can you get honey from the dead body of Mussolini? Or, as Davenport put it, "What can survive as salvageable meaning from Fascism?" (p. 261). I do not think for one second, however, that Olson was interested in salvaging anything from fascism, or wondering if Pound could. He had not the slightest sympathy with Mussolini and had broken with Pound irrevocably in February 1948 when

Pound's fascist sentiments had become unbearably personal. Pound had scoffed at immigrants: "Ya, they'll end up in sterilization."[7] Olson went home and wrote his reply: "BUT you do have to deal with us Olsons, Leite-Rosenstock-Huessys: your damn ancestors let us in. (AND . . . I DON"T THINK THE BATHTUB WAS SO CLEAN WHEN THEY DID.)"[8] Pound had also scorned William Carlos Williams's mixed ancestry, which he said included "some jew from Saragossa."[9] Olson wrote in "GrandPa, GoodBye": "I left Pound that day and shall not see him again" (Seelye, p. 101). Olson would not end what he knew to be his first major poem with a question addressed to someone he never intended to speak to again.

If it is addressed to someone, there is a much better candidate. In sending the poem to Frances Boldereff on 26 October 1949, Olson commented that "the enclosed is in answer to a question you asked me one year and five months ago." He is thinking of a 26 June 1948 letter from her in which she requested: "tell me about America—tell me how it is for you." The question reverberated in his mind; he remembered it later in an intensified paraphrase as: "what, olson, do you see in these States to excuse them, tell me" (letter of 29 August 1953), referring in the same context to America as "this country which plagues us all." He took her to be saying the equivalent of "where maggots are, shall you uncover honey?" The question is Boldereff's if anybody's. But she is an entirely invisible presence in the poem, and there is a strong argument that she is not there at all. The fact that there was no mention at all between the two correspondents of anything concerning the development of "The Kingfishers" during the seventeen months from her request to his "answer" suggests that the poem was not caused by the question but, when finished, seemed to Olson to be something that could be sent as a reply.

There is a better candidate still: the poet himself. Olson often in diaries addressed himself as "you"; I think he is doing so here. "I pose you your question": this is not a reposing of a question already asked by a "you." It is a question to be posed now to a "you" who has become ready for it through the ruminations of the poem. Olson is asking himself what he can do to make something of the world he is in, no matter how rotten it may have become.

No, the maggots of the poem are an image of general decay, not Poundian maggots. But if we think of Pound here, Olson has only himself to blame. A few lines earlier he actually named Pound as his next of kin, in lines 176–79:

> But I have my kin, if for no other reason than
> (as he said, next of kin) I commit myself, and,
> given my freedom, I'd be a cad
> if I didn't. Which is most true.

This is a deliberate allusion to the cocky first page of Pound's *Guide to Kulchur:*

> It is my intention in this booklet to COMMIT myself on as many points as possible, that means that I shall make a number of statements which very few men can AFFORD to make, for the simple reason that such taking sides might jeopard their incomes (directly) or their prestige of "position" in one or other of the professional "worlds." Given my freedom, I may be a fool to use it, but I wd. be a cad not to.

"Which is most true"—Olson is approving of what he quotes from Pound.[10] Because Pound did say the words, there can be no doubt that it is he who is called "next of kin." Yet this is most surprising in view of the pains we have gone to to show that Olson disengaged himself from Pound in February 1948. How is it that Pound can now be brought into the poem in this favorable way?

The answer lies in what happened a year after Olson's break with Pound. In February 1949 a committee that included T. S. Eliot, Robert Lowell, Allen Tate, Conrad Aiken, and many others was canvassed by mail to decide on the best book of poems published in the previous twelve months. Pound was voted the $1,000 Bollingen Prize for *The Pisan Cantos*. Olson broke his year-long silence with a letter to Dorothy Pound on 24 February 1949: "Do tell the O. M. how delighted I am les autres up and did what they did, and make it clear to him that the award makes more sense to us, his sons, than all beribboned and laurelled junk he and others have measured progress by."[11] Despite the backhanded compliment at the end, this is a sincere greeting. When he terms himself a son (next of kin) he is simply acknowledging an objective fact of literary descent. But this would not have got Pound into "The Kingfishers" without what happened next, the uproar against Pound's getting the award. Robert Hillyer wrote "Treason's Strange Fruit" in the *Saturday Review of Literature* for 11 June

1949. Karl Shapiro, who had voted "No" on the committee, detailed his reasons in a special issue of *Poetry*. Most literary periodicals joined the furor. We do not know exactly at what point that summer Olson decided to commit himself on the Bollingen question publicly, for he did not write any letters to the editor or anything of that sort. What he did was to interpolate into part III of "The Kingfishers" at a late stage[12] a stanza declaring himself a son of Ezra's. He felt, given he had the same kind of freedom from professional constraint as Pound was referring to in *Guide to Kulchur*, he too would be a cad if he did not commit himself on the question. The intrusive stanza disturbed the clear flow, as he had it, of his tribute to Rimbaud, and the stitches made when the four lines were sewn in are not entirely invisible. But he had to do it. It is the first act coming after the struggle of the poem. He is, indeed, able to find a little honey in the dead carcass of his relationship with Pound. He might also have gained a small secret satisfaction in being able to think he had found a way, with the allusion to Pound, of finally bringing into "The Kingfishers" his weary Cabeza de Vaca; for when he was ruminating once again on "The Long Poem" on 27 May 1948 he had linked Cabeza and Pound together, asking: "Is Cabeza an equivalent Aeneas, emerging from the broken ant-hill of Europe?" (*OLSON* 5, p. 38).

IV

Saved until last are what might be considered the most perplexing lines in "The Kingfishers" (lines 172–75):

> I am no Greek, hath not th'advantage.
> And of course, no Roman:
> he can take no risk that matters,
> the risk of beauty least of all.

Some readers have not been perplexed, taking it that Olson is placing himself rather lower than the Greek and rather higher than the Roman—a nice balancing act. I agree about the Roman. The lines are leading up to the poet's felt kinship with Rimbaud, who can certainly be said to have taken the risk of beauty, and the further risk of tossing Beauty off his knee, as Olson put it.[13]

Where there is risk, there is the possibility of tragedy. Olson does not feel as courageous as Rimbaud in this regard, but he is no Roman, who, he says, avoids the risk of tragedy by taking no risk that matters. This is stated more specifically in the variant version sent to Caresse Crosby:

> I am no Greek,
> hath not th'advantage.
> And of course no Roman:
> who[14] can take no risk that matters,
> the risk of beauty least of all.
> Thus, and only thus, no tragedy.

Olson is painting with a large brush here, and I am not prepared to enter into an evaluation of his judgment about Rome and beauty. (It seems to be debatable, but I am not aware he debates it anywhere.) He is, he says, *of course* no Roman and gives the reason he does not feel kinship: the Roman has a certain deficiency. When we turn to "I am no Greek," which seems a more important and difficult issue, we have every reason to expect that the construction is in parallel: he is no Greek because the Greek too has certain disabilities. He does not feel kinship with the Greek, because he (the Greek) "hath not th'advantage"?[15]

Despite the fact that the "hath" requires a third person singular subject, most readers have felt that it must be the "I" of the poem who does not have the advantage. We (I include myself until I was forced to think about it more rigorously) have heard the line as a dying fall, like Prufrock's "No! I am not Prince Hamlet, nor was meant to be." We have heard the "hath" as a self-pitying lisp, and the tone as similar to "Maximus, to himself": "I have had to learn the simplest things / last. Which made for difficulties" (I. 52). This particular *Maximus* poem has become such an anthology favorite because we are still caught in the trap of the Romantic poet and his suffering. We like the mournful falling on the thorns of life; we find it comfortable, somehow appropriate. But we should be aware that Olson did not share these feelings. He did not value "Maximus, to himself" except as an exception, the one subjective soliloquy that he would allow into the total scheme of *The Maximus Poems*. He made this quite clear when Gerard Malanga asked him to read the poem onto tape near the end of the "*Paris*

Review Interview," where he calls the poem "weak": "I believe that in the present the subjective is so strong that, if you aren't willing to treat it as a weakness, you won't get anywhere. . . . And I just deliberately have fallen in on my face" (*Muthologos* 2, pp. 147–48). This is not just a casual self-criticism in passing; it leads to the central tenet of postmodernism: that we do not have to be at odds with ourselves or the universe, that we can come into our own. "Maximus, to himself," Olson told Malanga, "has the lesion of talking about myself, which I permit myself at this one point to let the leak in. . . . Otherwise, the boundaries have to be as tight as our structural—'moral structures'" (*Muthologos* 2, p. 148). Olson did not lisp. His normal mode of speech was emphatic. I do not think he is here saying, "Poor old me, I don't have the advantages the Greeks had."

Olson had read widely in Homer and Greek drama through the years. His great discovery had been Victor Bérard's work on the *Odyssey*, but the foundation for his sense of "the Greek" was undoubtedly Werner Jaeger's *Paideia: The Ideals of Greek Culture*, volume 1 of which he owned later in paperback. He had seen the 2d ed. which came out in 1945 from Oxford University Press and had read at least the first chapter, "Nobility and Areté." Jaeger defines the word "areté" as "proud and courtly morality with warlike valour . . . the quintessence of early Greek aristocratic education" (p. 5); to which he adds Aristotle's notion that "the highest areté" is "to take possession of the beautiful" (p. 12). The latter phrase, says Jaeger, is "so entirely Greek that it is hard to translate"; it is not aesthetic or spiritual but "moral heroism": "to abandon possessions and honours in order to 'take possession of the beautiful'" (p. 13). The Roman lacks this kind of heroism, says Olson in the poem, and so does not rate up there with the Greeks. But—and it is a big but—where can Olson rate the Greeks when their reaching out for beauty is mainly to do with military valor? On 11 May 1949 Olson drafted a poem he entitled "Ilias" (Unpublished poems file at Storrs), in which the whole Trojan War boils down to this:

> All the argument is a whore and a cuckold
> In which fools fight fools for each other's trash.

Olson is apparently not taken in by Aristotle's propaganda. The heroes of the *Iliad* take possession of trash not the beautiful.

He called Homer a "late" European poet and valued more the earlier writers of the Near East. Or he looked to the outsiders, like the Hittites. Charles Doria remembers that when in Buffalo he started exhibiting his classical education Olson said to him: "You are a Greek, I am a Hittite" (*boundary 2*, p. 134). Doria took that to mean that Olson considered himself "a hostile power who had preceded me and everyone else who had associated themselves with Hellenism" (p. 135). When Olson taught "Tutorial: the Greeks" at Black Mountain College in 1955, he warned the students to go both "backwards" from Ancient Greece and also "outside," and "not get caught in that culture trap of taking them [the Greeks] forwards, as tho all that we are depends on em" (*OLSON 2*, p. 45). Simply put, Olson's greatest achievement is to have postulated a postmodern moral structure that is an "alternative to the whole Greek system" (*Selected Writings*, p. 55). He continually asserts that what we will find useful for our future is other than what we have inherited from the Classical Greeks. For this reason, I consider it not possible that Olson's stance in the first line of part III of "The Kingfishers" involves acknowledging some advantage to the Greek worldview. It must be the other way round. He has not yet got to that wonderful assurance of "Maximus to Gloucester, Letter 27 [withheld]," where he states (II.14–15):

> No Greek will be able
> to discriminate my body.
>   An American
> is a complex of occasions,
> themselves a geometry
> of spatial nature.
>
>   I have this sense,
> that I am one
> with my skin
>
>   Plus this—plus this:
> that forever the geography
> which leans in
> on me I compell
> backwards I compell Gloucester
> to yield, to
> change

>   Polis
>   is this

Here in 1954 he characterizes "polis" as a problem an American faces that has a complexity the Greek could not understand. The Greek's "warlike valour" would be no advantage. Olson intuited this as far back as "The Kingfishers."

To read the line

>   I am no Greek, hath not th'advantage

in such a way that the poet, not the Greek, is advantaged is consonant with Olson's central thought. He would have made it quite clear if he had included a "he" and italicized it thus:

>   I am no Greek; *he* hath not th'advantage.

I believe that that is the thought that the line is meant to communicate. Unfortunately, the stubborn fact is that the line is not written with an italicized *"he."* The line is written in such a way that almost all of us have taken it, and almost all of us will continue to take it, that the "I" is the one who does not have the advantage. It is true: the line appears to have been written so that we should take it that way. If so, then we must insist that the poet is saying exactly the opposite of what he appears to be saying.

The word for this is irony. I believe Olson was being ironic. If we take the line to read something like

>   I am no Greek; one hath not th'advantage, doth one?

and with a rather arched tone, this might be exactly how Olson is asking us to read it. That the Greeks were far above us has been such a cliché. If you want to oppose the cliché deftly, you state it sarcastically with a sort of uppercrust accent—which may also be a slap at T. S. Eliot at the same time.

Olson used the obsolete "hath" in relation to Eliot in the draft of "Projective Verse," where he said, in the 6 February 1950 version sent to Frances Boldereff, that he was "going to try to set down the limits and advantages of, this day." Five days later he sent a draft where he spoke of "Prufrock," which "doth stem from Browning (?), certainly hath obvious relation back to the Elizs., especially to the soliloquoth; yet OMeliot is *not* projective, goeth by his personeth." He falls into the "—th" endings for comic effect, ridiculing Eliot for being tied to old forms. He did not go through with it in the final version of the essay, but we cannot put it past him to have brought in Eliot with "hath not th'advantage" at the end of "The Kingfishers" as a final satirical nod to the "Anti-Wasteland" aspect of the poem. If not Eliot, then he is mimicking the tone of someone of that ilk, in a light-hearted but serious way letting the reader know, if the reader can hear the irony, how little advantage he believes the Greeks really have, and how for the future before us we must hunt among stones elsewhere.

8
"The Praises"

I

Because Olson's poem "The Praises" is cut from the same cloth as "The Kingfishers," we should spend some time with it, both for the possible clues to "The Kingfishers" and for its own sake. It might, in fact, be considered the completion of the circle of thought left open at the end of "The Kingfishers." The draft of the long "Proteus," as reproduced in facsimile in Appendix G, has the part that became "The Praises" following sequentially after "I hunt among stones." At this stage it was ready to be cut off as a separate poem. But previously it was to have been the middle part of the long poem, as an untitled plan at Storrs indicates:[1]

I 1	He & the birds
	  Fernand
			hangover
			  change	

2	Mao &
	  the phenomenology of
	    the birds
			change, forward
			  from what has
			    rotted
				The E
				on the stone

3	Tradition,
	  & violence
			tradition,
			  & violence
				stone

4	the feed-back,
	  & person
		Heraclitus	brought back
			  to person	

II She who was burned more than half her body skipped out of death

Ammonius	1	The E,
		  & the nature of
		    thought
			the root of
			  positive change
				Thus begin the
				arithmetical, the
				mathematical
				praises

Pythagoras	2	science,
		  & secrecy
			the two condition,
			  & nature's law:
			    straightest possible process	

Pythagoras	3	the law of numbers		

8: "The Praises"

```
III 1  Avert, avert
       avoid pollution
       to be clean              general statement
       in a city
       O Wheel

    2  It is true, the light is  Am specifically
    3  the 2                     Quetzalcoatl & Cabeza
```

We sense that the "Praises" part would be affirmative. Part II of the outline refers to "the root of positive change," which begins "the mathematical praises." The world of change is harmonious, and growth is governed by laws, the mathematical expression of which has called forth the praises of thinkers. "Each one of the numbers," Plutarch says in Olson's source (King ed., p. 190), "taken by itself will furnish much scope for such as wish to praise it." Taking "The Praises" for the title cannot be other than indicating the traditional gratification to be found in solutions to problems.

The continuing problem is to "know thyself," and though the Delphi E does not appear in the published version of "The Praises," it was there in typescript drafts, indicating the connection with "The Kingfishers:"

> To be very very timid or, what amounts to the same thing, very shrewd[2]
>
> Comes E, comes the five, and afterwards
> the rage of song
>
> Comes E, comes the five, and afterwards
> on the sixth day of the new moon
> at the first casting the three lots
> you throw neither deuce nor three,
> and the reason must not be divulged.
> Thus is concluded the arithmetical, the mathematical
> praises.
>
> She who was burned more than half her body skipped out of death

—most of which comes from the King ed. of Plutarch (p. 189), where the discussion of the E at Delphi in its significance as the number five is conducted.[3] Because of this evidence that Olson paid attention to the numerical harmony aspect of the E, when in line 24 of "The Kingfishers" he says he "thought of the E on the stone" we should to some extent take the whole import of "The Praises" to be present.

The last line of the quoted passage, the reference to the burnt woman, is the first line of "The Praises" as published. We do not know if this was a newspaper item or Olson's personal knowledge, probably the latter.[4] In any case, anonymity is appropriate here, for the woman stands as an example—an extreme example—of the mathematics of life and death. The body can resist a certain percentage of burn, which can be precisely known. This concept leads into Olson's chief source for "The Praises," Matila Ghyka's *The Geometry of Art and Life* (New York: Sheed & Ward, 1946). In the introduction to his book, Ghyka, a modern Pythagorean, states what his title implies: "There are then such things as 'The Mathematics of Life' and 'The Mathematics of Art,' and the two coincide" (p. xii). The flow of life—how can it be measured? What are the laws of change and continuity? How can we fix the real in its flux? These are questions "The Kingfishers" shares with "The Praises," the two poems having come into existence under the sign of "Proteus." How can you pin down the demigod of change? Behind the Homeric myth of wrestling with Proteus there lies a deeply imbedded notion that the essence of life involves a physical struggle that will reveal the laws of nature and being.

What are the operative laws of organic form that Olson finds in Ghyka? "We shall attack," says the poem (line 14 and following), by means of Bonacci's series, as one finds it exhibited in nature. Life cannot help but take mathematical ratios: "Pendactylism is general in the animal kingdom" (line 25). All this section of the poem is right out of Ghyka (though Olson mistranscribes Ghyka's correct "pentadactylism"):

> The pentadactylism (five fingers, or corresponding bones of cartilages) general in the animal kingdom is a manifestation of the same predominance of the number 5 and pentagonal symmetry. We will see . . . that this predominance is indeed a characteristic of living forms and living growth. (pp. 18–19)[5]

Olson has turned to Ghyka for the same reason he got immediately on the scent of Wiener's cybernetics: there are laws here for the

8: "The Praises"   111

human universe. Ghyka's plate XLI (p. 109) diagrams the male body, somewhat like Leonardo's akimbo figure in a circle, but with more complicated mathematics. Plate XLII is "Harmonic Analysis of Horse in Profile." Numbers themselves seem to explain the strength of what Olson in "The Resistance" essay called our "fragile mortal force" (*Selected Writings*, p. 14).

Olson was fond of quoting a saying from Novalis: "He who controls rhythm controls the universe."[6] The essential point of Matila Ghyka's *The Geometry of Art and Life* is that rhythm and number are the same. One sentence underlined by Olson reads (p. 5): "*Rhythmos* and *Arithmos* had the same root: rhein equals to flow." The numbers flow, poetry controls the universe, and thus the poet becomes of use. Olson found the Pythagoreans appealing because metrical structure was everything to them, as it is to the poet. That strange title, "The Praises," drawn from the Pythagorean "mathematical praises," can thus come to be seen—without Olson actually saying so—as honoring his own craft of poetry.

II

"The Kingfishers" begins with a hangover; it is a trifle edgy throughout. Olson did not really want to do more than stir himself into beginnings. He made sure that solutions did not come too immediately to hand. He reserved for "The Praises" some of the flow of energy that he could have used in the earlier poem but chose not to. Appendix C reveals one such postponed passage. The "whence it arose" (line 161 as it exists in isolation in "The Kingfishers" as published) was to have been followed by lines taking us into the human brain where "the old appetite" has its seat. Picked up for "The Praises," the lines lose their foreboding aspect. It is now love that arises from the "throne of bone" (lines 89–97):

> And you, o lady Moon, observe my love,
> whence it arose
>
> Whence it arose,
> and who it is who sits,
> there at the base of the skull, locked
> in his throne of bone, that mere pea of bone

> where the axes meet, cross-roads of the system
> god, converter, discloser, he will answer,
> will look out, if you will look, look!

Again, this stresses the physiology of action and will, for the pea of bone is none other than the pituitary gland, whose secretions control other glands and influence growth. Here is the "god" (with a small *g*) of change, or "the captain? stabilizer?" as Olson put it in "mythography and geometry" notes at Storrs. A Storrs note dated 7 March 1949 refers to "the pituitary as source of the electric will . . . which penetrates all horizontals of acquired material and which keeps in constant being the archaic or primordial." This is the center of the archaic in each person, which, in Olson's notion of the postmodern, gives us the felt sensation of being at home in the universe. This god-in-us, the converter of events into experience, the soul tissue that discloses ourselves to ourselves in consciousness, this will answer, if we ask. This is a riveting expression of self-reliance and confidence in our will to change.

Not all of the obscurities in "The Praises" can be taken up meticulously here; however, insofar as the poem may be thought of as completing "The Kingfishers," its major themes will interest us (i.e., those expressing the methodology of accomplishment.) One might turn first to those beautiful lines 44–49, which have the form of Confucian analect, but since no source has yet been found may really be Olson's own pituitary speaking.

> Sd he:
>   to dream takes no effort
>   to think is easy
>   to act is more difficult
>   but for a man to act after he has taken thought, this!
>   is the most difficult thing of all.

Our two poems together are a man taking thought about what it would mean to be of use.

> It is the use, it is the use
> you make of us, the use
> you make of
> you!

8: "The Praises"

These four lines ended "The Praises" in its first printing. They were presumably considered overemphatic and deleted from later reprintings.[7] We include them here for their emphasis. Olson is concerned "that that which has been found out by work may, by work be passed on / (without due loss of force)[8] / for use / USE" (lines 116–19). Thus speaks the man who has been hunting among stones.

It is the work ethic that is at the pituitary of Olson's psyche, the New England immigrant psyche. In the very first entry of the notebooks at Storrs we hear the young intellectual worker at the threshold of life, 1 March 1932:

> Emerson's "American Scholar" has inflamed me again. As a Phi Beta I pledge myself to that philosophy of life, a life, not of pedantry, but of service and success, through nature, thought and action—Man Thinking and Man Living. It is because of, not the honor, but the responsibility of Phi Beta Kappa that I sent for my golden key yesterday.

Behind this high ambition is the image of the worker, which Olson invokes more than once in the shape of his Irish grandfather, who

> rolled in the grass
> like an overrun horse
> or a poor dog
> to cool himself
> from his employment
> in the South Works
> of U S Steel
> as an Irish shoveler.[9]

That was his mother's side. His father and the dignity he brought to his job as a letter carrier are the subject of the long short story, "The Post Office," written just before "The Kingfishers." A notebook entry of 8 March 1948 exhorts the writer to "do this book on yr father without reference to culture—style, manner, tricks—do it on the level of mediocre humanitas."[10] This desire not to make a hero out of his father was, naturally, doomed to failure, because Olson could not help but believe that work "done right" is heroic:

> We have forgotten what men crave. We think that all workers want is pay. But that's all they are left with, where production, and that rot of modern work, efficiency, rule. . . . My father was old fashion. He had notions having to do with courtesy, modesty, care, proportion, respect. (*The Post Office*, p. 47)

Olson's father carried these five qualities (like Sir Gawain's shield) into battle against the bosses. He was like Antiochus with his dream of the pentagram ("The Praises" lines 8–13, taken from Ghyka p. 114):

> whence Alexander
> appearing in a dream to Antiochus,
> showed him
> And on the morrow, the enemy (the Galates)
> ran before it,
> before the sign, that is.

Charles Olson Sr. was a union officer fighting for quality service against the route inspector and the dehumanizing efficiency that came to dominate the workplace after World War I: "We have got so used to change that we are unwilling to believe that suddenly some change may be so total as to destroy. The path does die" (*The Post Office*, p. 44). The jungle leaps in.

As a more objective correlative for the worker of fortitude, Olson made early and continued use of the figure of the carpenter, not in the Christian aspect, but as a sincere workman: "the carpenter obeyed topography and a sense of / proportion: as a hand addresses itself to the care of plants"—as Olson had it in a poem "Elegy," dated 5 June 1947,[11] where the carpenter is the anonymous builder of New England clapboards. Very soon he could give a name to him, out of his newly acquired copy of J. J. Babson's *History of the Town of Gloucester* (1860): "William Stephens, shipwright," adding from p. 165: "more regard to his substantial performance than the wages he was to receive, and soe grew to poverty."[12] "That carpenter is much on my mind," says "Letter 7" of *The Maximus Poems*. "I think he was the first Maximus" (I.31). Butterick's *Guide to the Maximus Poems* lists several more references in the poem to Stephens as a hero, like the poet's father, one who worked with courtesy, modesty, care, proportion, and respect. Again, somewhat like his father, Stephens was "fined, imprisoned, and deprived of his privileges as a freeman for firmly speaking against royal interference in local government" (*Guide*. p. 50).

> . . . his remarks
> to officers of the Crown
>
> which were considered
> seditious (as my own Father's
>
> remarks to Paddy Hehir
> and to Blocky Sheehan
>
> were considered
> insubordinate.
>
> (*Maximus* III.30)

This is the courage that makes Olson say of Stephens that "he founded Troy / on this side of history" (III.29). With similar courage Apollonius of Tyana stood up to the Emperor Domitian, saying that there is always "the moment that suits wisdom best to give death battle."[13]

III

Courage is always a problem for ingenious and resourceful intellectuals, who tend to find ways to dodge danger and leave courage unexercised. But Olson (despite line 184 of "The Kingfishers") had his moments. One of them was at Black Mountain College when he faced off against that well-known wizard of the pentangle, Buckminster Fuller. When Olson arrived at BMC in October 1948, they were still talking about Bucky's geodesic dome of the previous summer. Both of them were there for summer 1949; there were the makings of a head-on collision. Martin Duberman in his *Black Mountain* book has described Fuller "launched into his mesmerizing monologues" ("man has now completed the plumbing and has installed all the valves to turn on infinite cosmic wealth"[14])—this would be provocative to a poet who rather preferred the plumbing not to work perfectly and who saw wealth as no aim either for himself or society. "Although each man was looking for a comprehensive view of the twentieth-century world," says Harris, "Fuller's belief in technology as a solution to contemporary problems was anathema to the postmodernist position Olson was beginning to formulate" (p. 163). "The Kingfishers" was fine-tuned and sent off for publication on 20 July 1949; it is interesting to speculate that the left-over material might never have been given form as "The Praises" if Buckminster Fuller had not shown Olson the typescript for his "Untitled Epic Poem on the History of Industrialization." Fuller has said that Olson became very excited. No wonder. This was a long work of quickly composed, chopped prose, extolling the principle of efficiency through mechanization of the world. Ironically, it was Olson's protégé Jonathan Williams who later published Fuller's book-length poem in the Jargon series, at which time Williams received a stern letter about "your horrifying news that you had had anything to do with Buckminster Fuller, and especially that epic which he had brought out of a safe to ask me to read that long ago back there in Old Carolina."[15] The crisis came, according to the story as told by Olson in conversation, when it seemed as though the future of Black Mountain would go either in Olson's direction or Fuller's. Fuller came to Olson's house on campus "with his men" for a confrontation; he went in the house alone with Olson for an hour; then he came out and took his men off to New York. Commenting on this to Creeley in a letter of May 1952, Olson said: "I drove Buckminster Fuller out of my house here three years ago come summer by saying to that filthiest of all the modern design filthers: 'In what sense does any extrapolation of me beyond my finger-nails add a fucking thing to me as a man?'" (*Creeley Correspondence* 10, p. 68). This rout might be called, using lines 104–6 of "The Praises," "the dispersion which follows from / too many having too little / knowledge." I do not think it belittles the poem to see behind it a rivalry for "political power" of this order.

> And they took over power, political power in Gr Greece, including
> Sicily, and maintained themselves, even after the Master died, until,
> at Metapontum, the mob
>
> "Only Philalaos, and Lysis, did not perish in the fire. Later,
> Archytas it was, pupil of Philalaos, who, friend to Plato,
>   initiated him,
> and, at Tarentum
>
>   (lines 120–25)

8: "The Praises"

Fuller came to Black Mountain with twelve disciples from the Institute of Design in Chicago who were felt by some to be aggressive and "of a business sensibility" (Harris, p. 160) in conflict with the meditative life of the college. The battle, or the private duel, or exorcism, or whatever it was, seems to have produced the desired effect:

> by shipwreck, he perished (Hippasus, that is)
> the first to publish (write down, divulge)
> the secret
> the construction of, from 12 pentagons,
> the sphere
>
> "Thus was he punished for his impiety"
>
> (lines 108–13)[16]

Olson follows immediately with: "What is necessary is /containment" (lines 114–15). In the "Projective Verse" essay Olson wrote of how the poet must be "contained":

> If he sprawl, he shall find little to sing but himself, and shall sing, nature has such paradoxical ways, by way of artificial forms outside himself. But if he stays inside himself, if he is contained within his nature as he is participant in the larger force, he will be able to listen, and his hearing through himself will give him secrets objects share. (*Selected Writings*, p. 25)

Containment has to do with secrets, holding them, not letting them out in a way that dissipates them wrongly. A whole section of "The Praises" (lines 50–72) is Plutarch's account of the four degrees of initiation into the society of the knowledgeable, the knowers of secrets. "What is related must remain enigmatic" (line 70)—otherwise, everything would be too obvious for words. In our own time there are just too many words for the obvious. We live in a confessional era. It now behooves us to take care to leave things covered. To use Olson's word for "modesty," it is *pudor* that is offended when things are divulged without the proper form of containment.

> What has been lost
> is the secret of secrecy, is

> the value, viz., that the work get done, and quickly
> without the loss of due and profound respect for
> the materials.
>
> (lines 98–102).

After sending "The Praises" to Frances Boldereff on 16 December 1949, Olson wrote a follow-up letter on 10 January 1950, in which he explained:

> Pudor, and containment: the secret of secrecy *is* some law of life, and it has to do with how the things we put into ourselves (of emotion as well as of experience, knowledge) *do* grow roots, stick their little feet down into the soil of the soul, and quickly, and that it abrogates this human knowledge (the instinctive knowledge of the secret) to have others expose in public something where the roots and the dirt around them have been shaken off.

We see from this that the little poem "These Days" (previously quoted) is not to do with exposing the roots but with protecting them in their authentic original cover so that they can be approached and considered. "Containment" is a word Olson used later in a poem "For Sappho, Back" to describe the way a dancer "contradicts / the waste and easy gesture, contains / the heave within, within" (*Collected Poems*, p. 162). There is, therefore, no reason (despite von Hallberg, p. 27) to think of the poet co-opting the current jargon of American foreign policy, George Kennan's theory of the containment of communism.

IV

"Which brings us to what concerns us in the present inquiry": with line 73, Olson introduces the ritual of aversion, the climactic point in "The Praises" as outlined on a sheet of paper in the "Kingfishers" file at Storrs:

THE PRAISES	(astringence the graphic & tangible
1 The E Delphi the enigmatic humilitas	(only from enigma, aversion, & secret can come consonant order)

8: "The Praises" 119

2 The Pythagorean
   the 5

                1 the enigmatic—the E—no dogmatism
3 avertive   because a man inevitably remains
   the false corruption   obscure to himself

                                                  burning
                2 the virtue of secrecy   pine
                   the 5—the mind, &   burned
                   harmony   she who was
                                            & wheel & bird
                3 the necessity of the   gong
                   avertive—to purify—
                   purge—the *wheel*, the
                   gong, the *bird*

In the final poem we do not get the gong, bird or pine (though they were given a working in Appendix G part IV), but we do get, in lines 74–78:

    Avert, avert, avoid
    pollution, to be clean
    in a dirty time
                O Wheel, aid us
                to get the gurry off

—where "gurry" is a nice Melvillean word, defined in chapter XCIV of *Moby-Dick* as "the dark, glutinous substance which is scraped off the back of the Greenland or right whale and much of which covers the decks of those inferior souls who hunt that ignoble Leviathan." For the Wheel as purifier Olson was drawing on the Egyptian and Orphic view, as found in Jane Harrison's *Prolegomena to the Study of Greek Religion* (Cambridge: Cambridge University Press, 1908), pp. 590–91. In the same volume, he found reference to "ceremonies of riddance" and "gods of aversion" (pp. 8–9), and also the following (p. 10), which he must surely have noted: "Greek religion contained two diverse, even opposite, factors: on the one hand the element of *service*, on the other the element of *aversion*. . . . The rites of service were of a cheerful and rational character, the rites of aversion gloomy." So first there is the gloom of aversion:

        You would have a sign. Look:
        to fly? a fly can do that;

> to try the moon?[17] a moth
> as well; to walk on water? a straw
> precedes you.
>
> (lines 79–83)

A typed note at Storrs dated 4 August 1949 gives a slightly different phrasing: "Walk on water? You are not better than a straw. / Fly? A fly can fly." Then the draft swings round to something of a more "cheerful and rational character":

> Conquer your heart.
> Then you are doing something,
> may become somebody.

These earnest lines do not get into the final poem, but what we do get (lines 84–86) should equally be viewed as pertaining to "the element of service":

> O Wheel! draw
> that truth
> to my house.

The poem ends with two truths of service. The first is from Plutarch (p. 179):

> What belongs to art and reason is
>   the knowledge of
>   consequences.
>
> (lines 128–30)

The other is a quotation from Leonardo da Vinci's notebook, via Ghyka (p. 173):

> Every natural action obeys by
> the straightest possible process.

I take these references to art as a private tribute to the man who Olson would consider the likeliest contender against Buckminster Fuller, Corrado Cagli, Senor Bagatto of Appendix F. Just as "La Préface" was written for Cagli's first show, "The Praises" was finished to be read at the opening of Cagli's exhibition on 15 December 1949 in Washington, "Drawings in the 4th Dimension." Olson's long introduction, according to notes at Storrs, dwelt on what might be summarized by a phrase from "The Praises" (lines 101–2) as Cagli's "profound respect for the materials" and ended with an aversive reference to the path the world has taken, which "in its corruptings, led us to Hitler and Hiroshima." Conversely, what Cagli's show should do is "to lead you a little way along the purer direction of that path, to a humanitas eased out of contemporary narrows." Cagli, whose five drawings had joined Olson's five poems to make up the volume *Y & X* (1948), must have represented "the graphic and tangible . . . the 5—the mind, & harmony" (as the outline to "The Praises" above had it). He had early taught Olson the arcanum of the Tarot, from which secret can come "consonant order." The Pythagoreans gained strength from the knowledge of number, being thereby in touch with necessities in nature. Now Cagli is initiating Olson into the geometry of the fourth dimension. Radical non-Euclidean mathematics joins archeology and depth psychology in forming the laws of the new human universe of the postmodern. It is a compelling conjecture that "The Praises," while warning us about a plausible popularizer of the dead end of modernism called Buckminster Fuller, is as a subtext praising Cagli for putting mathematical knowledge to proper use by containment in the right artistic form, one of the violets of the postmodern beginnings.

9
"The Kingfishers": Epilogue

I

When Olson spoke at the 1949 Cagli show about the path to a "humanitas eased out of contemporary narrows," he was leading to the *piece de resistance* of the occasion, "The Kingfishers," which he called "a presentation of a like world of my own" to place alongside Cagli's "Drawings in the 4th Dimension" so that "reality can be freshly seen." His notes for his introduction indicate he was planning to explain this as follows:

> Let me pose it my way: we are fixed in space, but if time is imagined as capable of all use at any given moment, then we can, and this is the advantage, comprehend in one action all that is inside and outside an object. And if that is true, if we can take up that power, then we can go further and understand such other less plastic, but still plastic things such as an event, an experience, a person.

Events, experiences, persons: to understand history and our place in the world, this in a phrase is the aim that "The Kingfishers" is a beginning of. A sign that the postmodern is taking over from the modern is that a new way of looking at history increasingly presents itself. "If you and I see the old deal as dead," Olson wrote to Creeley on 9 February 1951, "there is bound to be a tremendous pick-up from history other than that which has been usable." He mentions Sumer and the Yucatan (from where he is writing the letter, placing himself outside "the direct continuum of society as we have had it,"—*Selected Writings*, p. 84). And then he asks, "What from the present push out and back is going to stay as fixes ahead? the problem of such references is one gd nuisance"; and adds: "still think the use of such in Kingfishers the best try so far, the subtracting of, the too precise geographical or historical

9: "The Kingfishers": Epilogue 123

locatings" (*Creeley Correspondence* 4, pp. 132–33). According to this last remark, Olson seems thankful that he has not been too forward to state the particulars of his animus by firmly attaching easily recognizable bits of history and location. If he had said, "I am in Washington, D.C., the center of the rotting Western civilization and, along with Owen Lattimore and other named scholars, have seen the Far East changing with the Long March, the People's Congress, etc."—it would not have helped to make the point. Worksheets show the poet trying to be more specific about what constitutes the "gurry" we are in, but it did not work. He believes in particulars but not necessarily blatantly obvious particulars. The penalty of openness is to keep everything outside; it is the advantage of secrecy that the curious may find a way to be invited into one's domicile.

Explicators are not governed by rules of containment. Indeed, our hippocratic oath requires us to ask for the flat, prosaic answers. M. L. Rosenthal managed to get some such from Olson when the poet said in a letter that "The Kingfishers" was "an examination-confrontation of *America* as such versus predictions of & from the *East Wind*" (*Guide*, p. xxvi). All right, the poem is about America. The maggots are here; America is putrifying. It was brutalized from the start by a conquistador who predicted ourselves and our pejorocracy. How can we reverse the situation? How can we get some sweetness and light out of it? One, we can look for the most creative, energetic political model available. For Olson in 1949 this was China. Two, we can study the origins of American history and face up to the offenses against the aboriginal populations, and the cannibalistic-genocidal impulses involved. Three, we can look long at our own society until it reveals its shamefulness, and search for something other than what we have had from Greece and Rome to rectify our stance toward the future. Lastly, as individuals, we can try to understand our changing natures and enduring moral structure, to offer resistance to any change but the change we will into being. The poem, in my understanding of it, is a thoughtful response to the problem of being a sensitive American.

It is also a frustrated one. Olson agreed with someone who saw him as "an angry man" in this poem (letter to Frances Boldereff 20 August 1950). It was, as we have seen, a poem that had taken on Boldereff's question of how can one "argue survival in these

States"—how, in effect, can one stand to live there at all. On the eve of his departure for the Yucatan, about to distance himself for the first time in years from Washington, D.C. (that invisible weight on "The Kingfishers"), Olson wrote as an American to the European Rainer Gerhardt (letter of 15 January 1951):

> I feel finished with the frame of my people—that is, as an urgent necessity for me to come to conclusion about it (CALL ME ISHMAEL, surely, was a document of that struggle. And so much of the verse—KINGFISHERS, e.g.) And I go off with an ease and a joy and a hunger which surprises and delights me!

"The Kingfishers" is now published, and Olson is allowing himself to feel the reward of having worked on it, having said something, having "come to conclusion" about the state of things.

Olson in that letter does not sound to me like a man who believes in "indeterminancy." According to a recent article, "Kinesis and Meaning: Charles Olson's 'The Kingfishers' and the Critics," Olson has, "with malice aforethought, written a poem that refuses to be translated into a discursive register."[1] That this for the author of the article is a sort of praise of the poem does not recommend a critical opinion that runs entirely counter to what I feel are Olson's intentions and accomplishments here. The present book has tried to demonstrate that "The Kingfishers" is, above all, discursive. As von Hallberg put it, Olson's is "a referential poetics: hence subject matter is primary . . . as central as it was to the poet-prophet" (p. 22). For the vatic poet the whole world is at stake, and communication an absolute imperative. We are not, as with much published verse, being asked to admire how stylishly the poet dodges matters of importance. With Olson there is a desire to be veridical that is positively Emersonian.

On 9 January 1950 Olson sent a copy of "The Kingfishers" in typescript, despairing to wait for publication, to his old friend Ben Shahn: "When it got written, I said to myself, 'This, if anything, belongs to the Shahns.'"[2] This is a striking reminder of the political content of the poem; for Shahn, a Lithuanian immigrant to the United States in 1906, had natural sympathies for the underdog and put his enormous artistic talent at the disposal of left-wing causes. Olson had worked with Shahn at the Office of War Information 1942–43 and collaborated on a pamphlet, *Spanish Speaking*

9: "The Kingfishers": Epilogue 125

Americans in the War (1943), a celebration of a visible minority. They worked together again in the 1944 election for the CIO Political Action Committee. "Every worker a voter" was the battle-cry: Shahn did the poster, Olson's job was to see that the slogan became an actuality.[3] Shahn's biographer writes of the period after 1947 as a difficult time for any artist who attempted to "maintain the political commitment and artistic ideals of the New Deal era": "his paintings and posters were cited as communistic. . . . He was investigated by the FBI and blacklisted."[4] Compared with Shahn, Olson was on the fringe of the left wing (though he did have a disturbing visit from two FBI agents).[5] Olson on his way to support Claude Pepper at the Democratic Party Convention in Philadelphia in July 1948 dropped in to see Shahn in New Jersey. Shahn, a solid Henry Wallace man, would have shamed Olson a little. This would be the sense in which "The Kingfishers" might "belong" to Shahn: he represented that constant push from the left to keep Olson honest. If he could present the poem to Shahn with a clear conscience, then it must be because it was on the right side, as Shahn would think of it, the side of the working class from which they both came. Olson would not deny his old comrade-in-arms a reading of the first line of the poem as the old-fashioned hope for the peoples of the world: "What does not change / is the will to change." In Vancouver in 1963, beginning a public reading of the poem, Olson quipped, "I never did know what that meant." When he sent the poem to Ben Shahn in 1950 we can be sure that he knew what Shahn would take it to mean, and that he was content that Shahn would so take it. For Olson did believe that there is something that "balks one" more than the "protean real one carries inside," and that is the reality outside, "against which one breaks oneself like a body, in battle . . . that reality over there, the Enemie!"[6]

II

The publishing history of "The Kingfishers" is briefly as follows. It was being worked on at least by February 1949, first as the longer "Proteus" and then with its own closure by the middle of March 1949. Olson let it rest for a while, giving himself to his visits to Black Mountain. When he finally felt he had finished what he called "The Kingfishers I & II" (i.e., really the poem as we now have it) by 20 July 1949, he sent it off to *Poetry (London)*. On 16 August 1949 he could write to Edward Dahlberg: "I have worked on The Kingfishers, Poetry London will publish the first two parts of it" (*Dahlberg Correspondence*, p. 104). On 10 September 1949, he sent the poem to Cagli in Rome for translation and publication in Edizione D'Argo.[7] Then there was a setback. Writing to Vincent Ferrini and his wife from Washington on 6 October 1949 (letter at Storrs), Olson vented his spleen:

> i was blasted, on arrival, to find that those goddamn british had failed me again the kingfishers, which i value more than anything i have written, a long piece of verse, had, i understood, been taken by poetrylondon but here it sat, squat in the mail box, like odure, with a rejection slip over it, as civilized odure is always covered, from one of the editors who signed himself "gd," asking for something shorter instead shit.

It was apparently Monroe Engel who got *Hudson Review* to request a look at "The Kingfishers." To him the poet sent a carbon copy of the poem on 9 January 1950, the top copy "to go to the HUDSON . . . the going, of yr devising": "now that it goes, my poem, out again, i am full of anxiety for this time it must make it, or i shall cry down my country." He had also been putting "The Praises" into its own independent shape for the Cagli show of 15 December 1949, and sent a typescript to Henry Murray on 29 December 1949: "This locked itself up today (after eight months!). . . . I send it instead of 'The Kingfishers' because I hope, soon, to have that to send you in print." "The Praises" he sent off to *Western Review*, the only place that had proved itself to be hospitable to Olson's poetry;[8] "10 days ago i sent THE Ks mate, THE PRAISES, to West," Olson wrote in the 9 January letter to Engel; "by god he writes me right back, 'indeed i do like it, and will use it' jeezus, is that gratifyin', in the wilderness of this job!" But West ran into opposition from other members of the editorial board of the *Western Review* and had to return "The Praises." *Hudson Review* rejected "The Kingfishers." "What a time, and a game, this is!" Olson wrote to Engel on 3 February 1950; "the funny thing is, the assurance stays, i am cool." He sent "The Kingfishers" off to Robert Payne, who he knew wanted it for the first issue of his *Montevallo Review*.[9] It was finally published there in the first week of June 1950. "The Praises" went off to James Laughlin for his *New Directions* annual and appeared in the 1950 issue (No. 12) in January 1951.

III

We are here looking back at an age when Olson could only get his poems published because there was a wonderfully permissive and eclectic editor like Laughlin and a personal friend who was starting a magazine at a small women's college in Alabama. The 1950s were a time when things were simpler in the world of poetry. I remember Robert Frost telling a group of us that when poets sent him their volumes the ones that had rhymes and stanzas he kept, and the others he sent to Carl Sandburg. Given that choice, it was easy for us. Aided and abetted by the principles of New Criticism, we found our loyalties with poets such as Richard Wilbur and Donald Hall, gracious, witty, neat, like Robert Frost. It was bucolic while it lasted because it was an essentially aesthetic displacement. Our joy in appropriate imagery displaced the real content and rhythms of life. Anyone who subscribed to *Poetry New York* in 1950 (none of the people I knew did) would have read in "Projective Verse" a call to see things differently, to look out into the world and bring the world's energy into the poem through the poet's kinetic: "It is a matter, finally, of OBJECTS, what they are, what they are inside a poem, how they got there, and, once there, how they are to be used. . . . Objectism is the getting rid of the lyrical interference of the individual as ego, of the 'subject' and his soul" (*Selected Writings*, pp. 20, 24). These were radical and stirring words for someone who was ready for them. Projective verse, said Olson, proposes a "stance toward reality," which is a matter of content, what subjects the poet turns to and "the scale in which he imagines that matter's use" (*Selected Writings*, p. 24). The scale will be large, or at least "projective"; one will project oneself, as in an opera house, so that every whisper or shout will be heard because of the energy that is belonging to each. "Projective Verse" was liberating and inspiring.

Few heard it as such until the essay, along with "The Kingfishers," was reprinted by Donald Allen in *The New American Poetry: 1945–1960*. Even then, some of us were slow to catch on to the fact that a really new and valuable idea had come into being. I myself edited a magazine in which John Simon did a scoffing review of the Allen anthology. Little did I know that Charles Olson would become my colleague in the English Department at Buffalo for an overlapping two years and cause me to see that what we were offering students in the modern field was a false currency. I began to feel that our attachments to certain modern writers had been largely sentimental or thinly aesthetic. It is not my purpose to disparage other writers to try to make Olson look brilliant, but simply to say that with "The Kingfishers" and its attendant "Projective Verse" a new kind of value seems to have come into being. This value will not be easily described, and I have surely not given in this book the impression that it can be. It will be easier known once the poem itself is understood for what it really is: an essay on the challenge of bringing new value into being.

Nobody has suggested that "The Kingfishers" is the last word on anything. It is more like the first word. As Olson told Cid Corman in a letter of 3 July 1951, "If you don't know Kingfishers you don't have a starter!" (*Corman Correspondence* I, p. 177). But he was already telling Frances Bolderelf in a letter of 13 July 1951: "I would now rewrite certain passages in THE KINGFS!" The context for this remark is illuminating. He had just been reading Jane Harrison's *Prolegomena to the Study of Greek Religion*, a passage about the chthonic snake that reminded him of a documentary film he had once seen about priestesses of a sect in India "who, once a year, have to kiss the snake at the mouth of his cave—and succeed by out-dancing, with the head, his thrusts, until he has spent the poison in his fangs, and they are able to touch his mouth with their mouth, at which he goes back into his crevice in the holy rocks." Which leads Olson in the letter to think of Zeus in his role as the Snake as well as the Thunderer:

> the importance of the DOUBLE, of the two-faced nature of things, throughout Nature, the ambiguity of reality, to restate it because all rational thot, the lie, has raised up the generations to think there is ONE, and thus the burdens of choice, when, in actuality, there are ONE PLUS, which is sufficiently dramatized in TWO, in the binary.

It is then he says he would rewrite certain passages in "The Kingfishers." He does not specify which. Perhaps it might be the emphasis on "This very thing you are" as a one. When he wrote later in a *Maximus* poem, "people / don't change. They only stand more / revealed," it could be implying that apparent differences are not development but the further illumination of the binary in us.[10] As time went on it seems that Olson began to feel that there were more things in heaven and earth (and under the earth) than were dreamed of in this poem's philosophy.

In February 1953, when Olson was stretching himself to pull off an Institute of the New Sciences of Man at Black Mountain College, standing up once more to ask "What is man?," he asserted the assumption "not only that he can be known, but that he need have none of the old fear that, known, what matters—the life in him—is in any way diminished."[11] This belief counteracts any previous worry that the quantum uncertainty principle should be extended into the human universe. This was a modernist worry, and modern writers in general fed off a sense of alienation, whereas "any POST-MODERN," as Olson put it in a letter to Creeley of 20 August 1951, "is born with the ancient confidence that, he *does* belong" (*Creeley Correspondence* 7, p. 115). In the same positive way Olson goes on in this New Sciences lecture to make, in effect, an amendment to "The Kingfishers," noting that "the E on the stone at Delphi from which Socrates drew his essential injunction—'Know thyself'—actually was a late and overt reading of the first E (on wood) on that site," and that the meaning of that earliest E is now known. "The meaning," says Olson, "can be put in this hieroglyph—'Man rejoicing!'"

Given this accretion of meaning, we can interpret better what Olson said when in Vancouver he stopped reading "The Kingfishers" after exactly one hundred lines: "I'm not with that one. I wrote this before I got into trouble." He is being ironic again. The "trouble" is likely to do with having reached a plateau where one can speak of "man rejoicing." It could have to do with the new commitment of his second marriage, or the experience of knowing himself "under the mushroom" with Timothy Leary, or doing the circumvallum of Ismaili angelology, or any of the other I Ching changes that were waiting for Olson in his later life. Most pertinent to "The Kingfishers" might be the conversion revealed in the marginalia of the poem's chief source, Plutarch's "On the E at Delphi." For instance, on p. 191 (the King ed.), attached to the quotation from Heraclitus about stepping in the same river twice, is the marginal note: "add Whitehead." Again, referring to "Reason distributes too much, dissolves and destroys" (p. 192) Olson writes: "right: correct via Wh's 10 seconds of the 'Actual' occasion." Against Plutarch's "*this* binds all existence together" on p. 194, he puts: "Wh's Consequence." Alfred North Whitehead's *Process and Reality*, which Olson used in spring 1955 before buying his own copy in February 1957, is a major intervention between the writing of "The Kingfishers" in 1949 and his being unable to finish a reading of it in 1963. Through Whitehead's *Process and Reality*, there is the possibility of a new stance, where the postmodern "archaic" receives addition from the religious sense of "primordial." "Whitehead has written the metaphysic of the reality we have acquired," Olson writes in *The Special View of History* (p. 16). "I call attention to Whitehead's analysis of the Consequent as the relative of relatives, and that the Primordial—the absolute—is prospective, that events are absolute only because they have a future, not from any past." Here the "projective" takes on new connotations from "my great master and the companion of my poems."[12] It is not our duty to exhaust this topic, only to remind ourselves that "The Kingfishers" is an early poem, written in the fourth year of Olson's life as a poet. There is another marginal note in the Plutarch volume (p. 191), against the following passage:

> the "yesterday" has died into the "today," and the "today" is dying into the "tomorrow," and no one remains, nor is *one*, but we grow up many around one appearance and common model, whilst matter revolves around and slips away.

The note reads: "1959, I wld know how much more true and relevant this is than I did in 1949 when K written."

In his twenty-first year as a poet, in a *Maximus* poem dated 11 February 1966, Olson seems to want to recall "The Kingfishers" (lines 114–115): "The message is / a discrete or continuous sequence of measurable events distributed in time." He wishes to add to the definition of "message" a quite new depth of meaning coming from his recent reading of Henry Corbin's *Avicenna and the Visionary Recital*, where in Avicenna's angelology it is the "Guardian" who "dictates" the message:[13]

9: "The Kingfishers": Epilogue

>   all does rhyme   like is the measure of
>   producing like, the Guardian
>   does *dictate* correctly the *message*
>   is a discrete and continuous conduction
>   of the life from a sequence of events measurable
>   in time   none of this *is* contestable
>
> (III.125)

The message is now where life is conducted with measure, dictated by the angel of order:

>   is the *Modus*
>   absolute? [I say it,
>   as a Prayer.
>
> (III.125)

He is no longer hunting among stones.

During the last year of his life, in an interview with a student who was lamenting that Black Mountain College had closed, the former Rector said the student had better just "do it" himself:

> Like in "The Kingfishers," which I wrote just at the time I was at Black Mountain. That's the point of the kingfisher—he lays his eggs in holes dug in banks. I mean, lay some eggs, for god's sake. Be fecund! Students, be fecund![14]

So Olson finally reveals, if we did not understand it before, that if the kingfishers in their "fetid nest" are a symbol of the gurry of the past and present, they are also, for their eggs, a symbol of the future.

Appendices

This book has not attempted to follow in detail the process of composition of "The Kingfishers" and "The Praises." To investigate a poet's choices and changes of mind often involves red herrings and tediousnesses that contribute little or nothing to an explication of the finished poem. In the body of the book I have tried to pick out of the worksheets bits of evidence that might justifiably make a difference to the way we see the poems. The following appendices include those few of the many drafts in the "Kingfishers" file at Storrs that may help elucidate those comments.

Appendix A. This is typed on the verso of the prose piece discussed in chapter 2(II). It is likely, however, that there were other worksheets intervening between the typing of the prose and the typing of these lines.

Appendix B. Transcribed and discussed in chapter 5(IV).

Appendix C. Discussed in chapters 6(III) and 8(II).

Appendix D. Discussed in chapters 6(III) and 7(II).

Appendix E. Discussed in chapters 4(III) and 7(I).

Appendix F. Discussed in chapters 4(III) and 7(IV).

Appendix G. This is the typescript of "Proteus" with Olson's holograph amendments from the "Kingfishers" file at Storrs, as presented by George Butterick in his *American Poetry* article (pp. 60–69). See his discussion (pp. 53–55).

Appendix H. "The Kingfishers" and "The Praises" as published.

APPENDIX A

What does not change / is the will to change

He woke, fully clothed, in his bed.
He could remember only the birds.
He had gone around the rooms when he came in,
and caught them, the green one first, with the bad leg
and the blue, the one they had hoped was a male.
Otherwise? Yes, Fernand.

Fernand had left without a word,
walking out of the room into his coat

Fernand, who had talked lispingly of Angkor Vat.
He had left without a word. Did anyone see him get up?
Or get into his coat? He was already out the door
When I saw him, he was at the door, all inside his narrows,
starting to slide along the wall of the night, to lose himself
in some crack of the ruins

What does not change / is the will to change

He woke, fully clothed, in his bed.
He remembered only the birds.
He had gone around the rooms when he came in
and caught them, the green one first, with the bad leg,
and the blue, the one they had hoped was a male.
Otherwise?
Yes, Fernand.

Fernand, who had talked (lispingly) of Albers, and Angkor Vat.
He had left without a word.
How had he got up, got into his coat? When I saw him
he was at the door, wrapped in his narrows, already
sliding along the wall of the night
losing himself in some crack of the ruins.

That it should be he who said, "Who cares for the kingfisher's feathers, now"!

Appendix B

IV

What you are / all is

a certain quantum, arrived at by accumulation,
which quantum, by that acuumulation, becomes
what all is, what you are, that which may
change

~~change~~; which better be understood to be
energy
given off
light is un proved
~~light~~, which ~~better be understood~~ to be
both particle and wave

what you are, what all is
uncertainty.... yet, uncertain
only in respect to when,
in what direction, where
you shall express yourself, burst

la lumiere,
la lumiere et la matiere
is one   l'amore
~~what matter is~~
is energy in
and out, is
constant, ~~if discontinuous~~
~~change,~~ is momentum solely
~~indeterminate only~~ in respect to
choice; ~~to the moment of~~
~~change, to the giving off of~~
~~light~~

It is necessary now to put it ~~another~~ this way:
the discontinuous is
the law, uncertainty is
the principle, nature
makes nothing but
jumps

We know now,
~~Let~~ Leibnitz holler, and go,
~~We~~ know now how we must act,
We know
what the eye is, how
he who rules us
converts, what it is
we must do :

to light and to matter
let one constant, 'h', be added,
to the five, to the E, let h be added,
~~and~though~as~as~to~this~day~~
let the h be added, even though, to this day,
it is susceptible of
no interpretation

let you be added,
let you be ~~that~constant~~
~~that constant~~, let you observe
in nature's sentence
that one undefinable syllable,
let you be

CHANGE

Appendix C

It is true. The light is
in the east. And we must rise,
act. Yet

in the west, despite the apparent darkness, the whiteness
which covers all, as
if you look, if you can bear, if you can, long enough,
as long as it was necessary for him, my guide
to look into the yellow of that longest-lasting rose,
so you must, and in that whiteness, into that face
                                      (what candor)
                                                   look
and,
considering the dryness of the place,
the long absence of an adequate rape

        of the two who first came, each a conquistador, no healer
        one healed, but the other tore
        the eastern idols down, toppled
        the temple walls which, says the excuser,
        were black with human gore

hear
where the dry blood talks
where the old appetite walks

        la piu saporita et migliore
        che si possa truovar al mondo
                                  (Viaggi, lib. 2, cap. 75)

where where it hides
look in the eye look! in the eye, how it runs
in the flesh, as chalk, but, under the petals,   the
in the emptiness) contemplate this light, regard/regard this light, contemplate
the inscrutable bulb of this hidden masker of flower the flower

    whence it arose, who sits
    locked in the bone, his min
    there in the skull, his that minute throne that pod
    that pod of bone looked at the crossroads of the mighty system
        , who rules   is
    at the precise point where the axis is in the back of the face where the axi
    where

    whence it arose, and who, also nobhocskull behind the face, sits there
    inckbocskull at the base of the skull, rules
    six the precise point where where the axes meet, at that precise point rest
    in his minute throne a mere pea of bone, at the crossroads, the god

Appendix D

V

It is true. The light is in the east. And we must rise, act. Yet
in the west, despite the apparent darkness, the whiteness
which covers all, if you look, if you can bear, if you can, long enough

        as long as it was necessary for him, my guide
        to look into the yellow of that longest-lasting rose

so you must, and in that whiteness, into that face
                                    (what candor)
                                                            look

and, considering the dryness of the place,
    the long absence of an adequate race

        of the two who first came, each a conquistador, one healed
        the other tore the eastern idols down, toppled
        the temple walls, which, says the excuser,
        were black from human gore,

hear, where the dry blood talks
    where the old appetite walks

        la piu saporita et migliore
        che si possa truovar al mondo

where it hides
look in the eye, how it runs
in the flesh, chalk, but, under these petals, in the emptiness
regard the light, contemplate
the flower

whence it arose

With what violence benevolence is bought
what cost in gesture justice brings
what wrongs domestic rights involve
what stalks
this silence

What pudor pejerocracy affronts
how awe, night-rest and neighborhood can rot
what breeds where dirtiness is law
what crawls
below

in this small-eared place
~~in the riot of this blood~~, in this blackness
~~what is the nature of~~
the light
can you find
light
shall the east uncover
enable you to recover
the light

        They bury their dead in a sitting posture

        serpent, cane, razor, path of the sun

```
            with her face to the west
            she sprinkled water (the midwife, that is)
            on the head of the child, crying
            "Cioacoatl! Cioacoatl!"
            and, the Mongolian louse
            in this thickness
            from what paradox act leaps out
            what honey is where maggots are
```

APPENDIX E

VII

In the juvescence of the year came dogwood, shadblow, STOP.
Avoid, avoid the priest. Avert
his droppings. Neither a bird nor a god, not the Fall of a sparrow,
but that simplest of things, an extraordinary man

in the juvescence came Cabeza not the least like a tiger
and we will speak of him, without gloss
but first, of this other, the predecessor, who came, likewise,
and against the weather, an extraordinary man

who died, or was immolated, April 5th, it turns out, 1208
who, in his life, did certain things which had value for
others

In the juvescence of the year he died, age 70, or thereabouts
if we are to judge from the fact that (1)   Knife
he started a year count in 1168, ~~tDayxlxYearxlxKnifet~~ calling it Day 1 Year 1 /
and,(2)

Appendix F

VI

I am no Greek,
hath not th'advantage.
And of course no Roman:
he can take no rish that matters,
the rish of beauty least of all.
Thus, and only thus, no tragedy.

But I have my kin, if for no ther reason than,
as he said (next of kin), I commit myself,
and, given my freedom, he went on,
I'd be a cad if I didn't.
Which is most true.

It works out this way, despite the disadvanatge.
I offer, as epigraph, a quote:
si J'ai du gout, xixxx ce n'est gueres
que pout la terre et les pierres.
For, despite the discrepancy (ocean courage age)
it is true: if I have any taste, it is only because
I have interested myself in
what was slain in the sun.

 otherwise,
To explain why it is, xii melodrama
I invoke one man, xxxxxxxxxxxxxxx he who was shipwrecked on this shore,
lost Europe's clothes, was naked how many winters,
lived on shell-fish, was torn by them, was slave,
first trader, learned what tribes these were, walked,
walked, found deer skin, clothed himself, walked
as the doe walks, white man, white, white
a second time

a second time, key to the opposite, xxxxxx rename him, Senor Bagatto
xxxxxxx a sceond time, and he only, of all, no one else, reborn!

I invoke you, conquistador. The rest xxxxxxxx were lies to myth
and, by a double-cross, created what? a state
but you, against the weather, bore out
the folk, against the weather did not kill
(where, among the stones, lies the tradition?)
you, and one predecssor who, at noon, in the highplace, refused
the blood (o man of flint,
and the sparrow's feather!)

I hunt among the stones.

Appendix G

THE FIRST PROTEID *The Kingfisher*
                                                          I + II

PROTEUS

1

What does not change / is the will to change

He woke, fully clothed in his bed. He
remembered only one thing, the birds
how, when he came in, he had gone around the rooms
and got them back in their cage, the green one first,
she with the bad leg, and then the blue,
the one they had hoped was a male.

Otherwise Yes, Fernand. Who had talked lispingly of Albers and Angkor !
He had left the party without a word. How he got up, got into his coat –
I do not know. When I saw him he was at the door. But it did not matter,
he was already sliding along the wall of the night,
in some crack of the ruins.
But it should have been he who said, "The Kingfishers! Who cares
for the kingfishers' feathers/now?"

His last words were, "The pool is slime". Suddenly, everyone,
ceasing their talk, sat in a row around him, watched
they did not so much hear, or pay attention, they wondered
looked at each other, smirked, but they listened.
he repeated and repeated, could not go beyond his thought,
"The Kingfishers' pool, the feathers were wealth, why
did the export/stop?" It was then he left.

2

I thought of the E on the stone, end of what Mao said:

la lumière
but the kingfisher
de l'aurore
but the kingfisher flew west
est devant nous!
he got the color of his breast
from the heat of the setting sun

The features are, the feebleness of the feet
(syndactylism of the 3rd & 4th digit)
the bill, serrated, sometimes a pronounced beak,
the wings where the color is, short and round, the tail
inconspicuous. But not these things were the factors. Not the birds.

The legends are legends. Dead, hung up indoors, the bird
will not indicate the approaching wind, or avert the thunderbolt.
Nor does its nesting. Still the waters, for seven days,
It is true, it does nest at the beginning of the year
but at the end of a tunnel bored by itself in the bank.

PROTY- 2

There, six or eight white and translucent eggs are laid,
~~but not on the bare clay~~ (thrown up in pellets by the birds. On these rejectamenta
(as they accumulate they form a cup-shaped structure)
the young are born, and, as they grow, this nest
of excrement and decayed fish, ~~brought for food~~,
~~becomes~~ a dripping, fetid mass.

Mao concluded:
nous devons
nous lever
et agir!

3

Then the attentions change, the jungle
even the stones are split. They rive.
Or later, that other conqueror
~~we more naturally recognize~~
he so resembles ourselves.

~~The note of the kingfisher is shrill. He is a solitary & pugnacious bird.~~
But the K/ qub so rudely on that oldest stone, sounded otherwise,
~~you~~/was differently heard. As, in another time, were treasures used
(and later, much later, a fine ear thought
a scarlet coat)

— // of green feathers, ~~with~~ feet, beaks, ~~and~~ eyes, of gold

¶ animals, likewise, resembling snails

¶ a large wheel, gold, with figures of unknown four-foots,
and worked with tufts of leaves, weight 3800 ounces

¶ last; two birds of thread and featherwork, the quills
gold, the feet gold
~~the two birds perched~~ on two reeds, gold, the reeds arising
from two embroidered mounds, ~~one yellow the other white,~~
and, from each reed, hung
seven feathered tassels.

In this instance the priests,
~~in dark cotton robes, and dirty,~~
their dishevelled hair matted with blood,
and flowing wildly over their shoulders,
rush in among the people, calling on them
to protect their gods.

And all now is war
where so lately there was peace,
end the sweet brotherhood of tilled fields.

PROTEE - 3

4
Not one death, but many
not accumulation but change, the feed-back proves, The feedback is
the law
Into the same river no men steps twice
                When fire dies, fire dies / No one remains, nor is, one.

Around an appearance, one common model, we grow up
many. Else how is it
to take pleasure now,
if we remain the same,
in what we did not take pleasure before? love
contrary objects.
admire and/or find fault
other words, feel other passions, have
nor figure, appearance, disposition, Tissue
the same?

To be in different states without a change is not a possibility.
We can be pleased. The factors is
It is possible now to be precise in the animal and the machine The factors:
the factors are
communication, and
control. Both involve
And what is the message. The message is
a discrete or continuous sequence of measurable events
distributed in
time

is the birth of air, is the birth of
water, is a state between the origin and
and the end, between the birth
and the beginning of
another fetid nest

is change, presents no more than itself; AM
the too strong grasping of it
when it is pressed together and condensed,
loses it,

This very thing you are

PROT ES - 4

II

It is true. The light is in the east. And we must rise, act. Yet
in the west, despite the apparent darkness, (the whiteness
which covers all) if you look, if you can bear, if you can, long enough

           as long as it was necessary for him, my guide
           to look into the yellow of that longest-lasting rose

so you must, and in the whitness, into that face
                                               (what candor)
                                                              look

and, considering the dryness of the place,
         the long absence of an adequate race

           (of the two who first came, each a conquistador, one healed
           the other tore the eastern idols down, toppled
           the temple walls, which, says the excuser,
           were black from human gore)

hear, where the dry blood talks
      where the old appetite walks

           la pix saporita et migliore
           che si possa truovar al mondo. (Viaggi,...)

when it hides, look
in the eye, how it runs
in the flesh; chalk, but under these petals, in the emptiness
regard the light, contemplate
the flower

whence it arose

           with what violence benevolence is bought
           what cost in gesture justice brings
           what wrongs domestic rights involve
           what stalks
           this silence

           that pudor pejerocracy affronts
           how awe, night-rest and neighborhood can rot
           what breeds where dirtiness is law
           what crawls
           below

2

I am no Greek, hath not th'advantage.
And, of course, no Roman:
he can take no risk that matters,
the risk of beauty least of all.

But I have my kin, if for no other reason than,

PROTEUS - 5

```
     as he said (next of kin), I commit myself, and
     given my freedom,
     Which is most true.

     It works out this way, despite the disadvantage.
     I offer, a quote:
     si j'ai du gout, ce n'est gueres
     que pour la terre et les pierres.

     Despite the discrepancy (an ocean  courage  ago)
     it is true: if I have any taste, it is only because
     I have interested myself
     what was slain in the sun

          They buried their dead in a sitting posture
          serpent  cane  razor  ray of the light sun

          And she sprinkled water on the head of the child, crying,
               "Cioacoatl! Cioacoatl!"
                                        the Mongolian louse.

          shall you uncover
          what honey is where maggots are

     I hunt among stones
```

PROTEUS - 6

to learn of the epiphanies, in this case, 4:

1st, to such as begin to learn and to inquire, he promises
the Pythian response, accompanied by the flute;

then, when part of the truth is glimpsed, he offers
the sun, or, as the Greeks imagined it, a creature of four-fold eyes,
and with four heads - of a ram a bull a snake and the bright-eyed l

But this little. For when a person has got the knowledge, Ammonius
(and he does not mean to be ambiguous) confers one overwhelming title:
he says a man can then call himself - OF THEBES.

The last and triumphant mode I shall leave as he leaves it, untranslat
When men are active, enjoy knowledge, that is to say, when they talk,
they are LESCHENOELEON.

And that said, Ammonius make clear why what is related must be enigma
to enjoy thought, says he, is to inquire, to wonder and to doubt;
to enter into the company of others is to inquire, to listen and to

From all this Ammonius excepts, of course, those who are entirely bru
not without soul. Which brings us to what concerns us in the present

2

Avert! avert! avoid
pollution
to be clean
in a dirty time

    O Wheel, aid us, to get the gurry off

Like pa does not like sis
on all detractors piss
o advertised earth
and you, O lady Moon, *shew my love,*
~~observe my love,~~
whence it arose

Come, wry-neck, sing
jugex, sing, jugex, jugex
to dirty ears

    O Wheel, turn, draw that truth
    to my house

My Sunday morning people, listen, hear

PROTEUS - 7

```
     the snake-bird   hiss
     "jugex, jugex"   and learn
     how to repel intruders
     from your selves
```

O Wheel!

O Goddess excellently bright
bless them with the wished sight
sing, cuckoo mate,
excellently sing,
jugex, jugex,
for light

Jean Vignot, before the city fathers, Milan, 1392, his answer
ARS SINE SCIENTIA NIHIL
when they asked him, master builder, what about the Dome

What has been lost is·
the secret of secrecy, the value, viz;
that the work get done, properly done, and quickly, without the loss of
due and profound respect for the materials

The which
is not so easy as it sounds, nor
can it permit the dispersion ######## which follows from
too many having too little
knowledge

         Sez Iamblichus:
by shipwreck he perished (Hippasus, that is)
the first to publish (divulge; write down, that is) the construction of
from 12 pentagons, the sphere. Thus was he punished
for his impiety.

What is necessary is
containment
in order that that which has been found out by work
may be passed on by work
without loss of its force
for use

         "And they took over power (political power, that is) in Gr Gr
including Sicily, and maintained themselves (even after the Mater died)u
at Metapontum, the mob

         "Only Philaleos, and Lysis, did not perish in the fire. Later
Archytas it was (pupil of Philaleos) who, friend to Plato, initiated him
at Tarentum, reestablished the State

Or, to put in another way, and to come to an occlusion equally hermetic:

PROTEUS - 8

you will know, so far as it is allowed to a mortal to know, that nature is,
from all points of view,
similar to itself

    (where the successive gnomons or differences are
    the integers of the natural series 1, 2; 3, 4,....., n
    representing, at the same time, the sum,
                            & the 4th triangular no.,
thus:

```
      .
     . .
    . . .
   . . . .
```

For what does not change, cannot, the invariant, is

    (L da V, his notebook)

every natural action obeys by the straightest possible process

4

whence it arose,
         and who it is, behind the face, who rules
who sits,
      there at the base of the skull, locked
in his throne of bone,
          (that mere pea of bone where the axes meet)
at that precise point of the crossroads of the system, god

he can answer, will look out
                      if you will look as long as it takes to find
out

   O-stone!   O E   O sing
        O E

5 Ὁλμείη
there are five solid figures, the Master concluded
(reports Aetius, in the *Placita*)
that the Sphere of the Universe arose
from the dodecahedron.

                   Whence Alexander
appearing in a dream to Antiochus
showed him, and, on the morrow, the Galates
(the enemy) ran before it.

EUS - 9

By Filius Bonacci, his series, rediscovered Pisa, 1202
we shall attack, for it, too, proceeds asymptotically towards
the graphic, and tangible, the law now determined to be ∮ phi

    its capital role in the distribution of
    branches, leaves, seeds (ex., the ripe sunflower)

    the ratios 5/8, 8/13 appear in the seed-cones of fir-trees,
    the ratio 21/34 in normal daisies

    & the reason is simple and instinctive:
    there is an ideal, and constant angle,
    for leaves and branches on a stem,
    which produces the maximum exposition to
    vertical light

    And pentadactylism is general in the animal kingdom
    but, among cystals, pentagonal forms or lattices
    do not, can not, appear

    Star and jelly fishes, sea-urchins, and, among flowers,
    fruit-blossoms, the briar rose, the honeysuckle
    campanulas; passion-flowers
    but lilies, tulips, the hyacinth, on the contrary, like cr

Sd. he:
  to dream takes no effort
   to think is easy
    to act is more difficult
  but for a man to act after he has taken thought
  this is the most difficult thing of all!

      IV

Nor is the halcyon bird a soverign specific against witches
of of any use in the wooing of a reluctant lady

Before the E let no woman epproach
let pine be the only wood burned
Before the E, let the incense be
the leaves of the bay alone
for here there are only two fates
where elsewhere there are three

The binary series is the law of choice
in man and, now, in the machine

Sound the gong! beware! beware! the bitches

PROTEUS- 10

are howling for us up and down the city!
the Goddess is at the crossways, sound the gong!
Sound
the apotrophaic gong!

Turn, turn away, obey
the Wheel!

Avoid, avoid the priest, Avert
his droppings. Neither a bird nor a god, not the Fall of a sparrow,
but that simplest of things, an extraordinary man

who died, or was immolated, April 5th, it turns our, 1208, who
in his life, did certain things which had value for others,

and brought about CHANGE!

He it is I now invoke, in answer to
our question:

he died, age 70 or thereabouts, judging from
(1) he started a year count in 1168 (May 1 Year 1 Knife)
and (2) he instituted a new fire cermony in Year 2 Reed.
(It was to be celebrated at intervals of 52 years)
He did not, of course, live to see it enacted a second time.
In a year 1 Reed, in the spring of that year, he died.
Or, at least, Venus did, that is, the planet
was last visible as the evening star April 5.
After an inferior conjunction with the sun, on the fourth day,
it is of some importance that, on the eighth, she reappeared:
look, in the morning sky, a star!
And that day, 1 Reed, became the day of his apotheosis.

And by that sign he was after known, and by it,
and by the sign of the Nine Wind, he is often shown
in that legendary place of origin,
the Seven Caves. So, that astronomer, that Toltec King,
possibly also himself a priest, QUETZALCOATL, he died.

And the plumed serppent reigns where the bird once flew.

Appendix H

THE KINGFISHERS

1
What does not change / is the will to change

He woke, fully clothed, in his bed. He
remembered only one thing, the birds, how
when he came in, he had gone around the rooms
and got them back in their cage, the green one first,
she with the bad leg, and then the blue,
the one they had hoped was a male

Otherwise? Yes, Fernand, who had talked lispingly of Albers & Angkor Vat.
He had left the party without a word. How he got up, got into his coat,
I do not know. When I saw him, he was at the door, but it did not matter,
he was already sliding along the wall of the night, losing himself
in some crack of the ruins. That it should have been he who said, "The kingfishers!
who cares
for their feathers
now?"

His last words had been, "The pool is slime." Suddenly everyone,
ceasing their talk, sat in a row around him, watched
they did not so much hear, or pay attention, they
wondered, looked at each other, smirked, but listened,
he repeated and repeated, could not go beyond his thought
'The pool the kingfishers' feathers were wealth why
did the export stop?"

It was then he left

2
I thought of the E on the stone, and of what Mao said
la lumiere"
       but the kingfisher
de l'aurore"
       but the kingfisher flew west
est devant nous!
       he got the color of his breast
       from the heat of the setting sun!

The features are, the feebleness of the feet (syndactylism of the 3rd & 4th digit)
the bill, serrated, sometimes a pronounced beak, the wings
where the color is, short and round, the tail
inconspicuous.

But not these things were the factors. Not the birds.
The legends are
legends. Dead, hung up indoors, the kingfisher
will not indicate a favoring wind,
or avert the thunderbolt. Nor, by its nesting,
still the waters, with the new year, for seven days.
It is true, it does nest with the opening year, but not on the waters.
It nests at the end of a tunnel bored by itself in a bank. There,
six or eight white and translucent eggs are laid, on fishbones
not on bare clay, on bones thrown up in pellets by the birds.

                      On these rejectamenta
(as they accumulate they form a cup-shaped structure) the young are born.
And, as they are fed and grow, this nest of excrement and decayed fish becomes
                      a dripping, fetid mass

Mao concluded:
       nous devons
              nous lever
                      et agir!

3
When the attentions change / the jungle
55 leaps in
            even the stones are split
                            they rive
    Or,
    enter
60 that other conqueror we more naturally recognize
    he so resembles ourselves

    But the E
    cut so rudely on that oldest stone
    sounded otherwise,
65 was differently heard

    as, in another time, were treasures used:

    (and, later, much later, a fine ear thought
    a scarlet coat)

            "of green feathers   feet, beaks and eyes
70   of gold

            "animals likewise,
            resembling snails

            "a large wheel, gold, with figures of unknown four-foots,
            and worked with tufts of leaves, weight
75   3800 ounces

            "last, two birds, of thread and featherwork, the quills
            gold, the feet
            gold, the two birds perched on two reeds
            gold, the reeds arising from two embroidered mounds,
80   one yellow, the other
            white.
                "And from each reed hung
                    seven feathered tassels.

    In this instance, the priests
85 (in dark cotton robes, and dirty,
    their dishevelled hair matted with blood, and flowing wildly
    over their shoulders)
    rush in among the people, calling on them
    to protect their gods

90 And all now is war
    where so lately there was peace,
    and the sweet brotherhood, the use
    of tilled fields.

4

Not one death but many,
95   not accumulation but change, the feed-back proves, the feed-back is
the law
> Into the same river no man steps twice
> When fire dies air dies
> No one remains, nor is, one

100   Around an appearance, one common model, we grow up
many. Else how is it,
if we remain the same,
we take pleasure now
in what we did not take pleasure before? love
105   contrary objects? admire and/or find fault? use
other words, feel other passions, have
nor figure, appearance, disposition, tissue
the same?
> To be in different states without a change
110   is not a possibility

We can be precise. The factors are
in the animal and/or the machine the factors are
communication and/or control, both involve
the message. And what is the message? The message is
115   a discrete or continuous sequence of measurable events distributed in time

is the birth of air, is
the birth of water, is
a state between
the origin and
120   the end, between
birth and the beginning of
another fetid nest

is change, presents
no more than itself

125   And the too strong grasping of it,
when it is pressed together and condensed,
loses it

This very thing you are

WHAT DOES NOT CHANGE

II

            They buried their dead in a sitting posture
130   serpent   cane   razor   ray of the sun

            And she sprinkled water on the head of the child, crying
            "Cioa-coatl! Cioa-coatl!"
            with her face to the west

            Where the bones are found, in each personal heap
135   with what each enjoyed, there is always
            the Mongolian louse

    The light is in the east. Yes. And we must rise, act. Yet
    in the west, despite the apparent darkness (the whiteness
    which covers all), if you look, if you can bear, if you can, long enough

140   as long as it was necessary for him, my guide
                to look into the yellow of that longest-lasting rose

    so you must, and, in that whiteness, into that face, with what candor, look

    and, considering the dryness of the place
        the long absence of an adequate race

145   (of the two who first came, each a conquistador, one healed, the other
            tore the eastern idols down, toppled
            the temple walls, which, says the excuser
            were black from human gore)

    hear
150 hear, where the dry blood talks
        where the old appetite walks

                            la piu saporita et migliore
                            che si possa truovar al mondo

    where it hides, look
155 in the eye how it runs
    in the flesh / chalk

            but under these petals
            in the emptiness
            regard the light, contemplate
160   the flower

    whence it arose

            with what violence benevolence is bought
            what cost in gesture justice brings
            what wrongs domestic rights involve
165   what stalks
            this silence

            what pudor pejorocracy affronts
            how awe, night-rest and neighborhood can rot
            what breeds where dirtiness is law
170   what crawls
            below

Appendices

III

        I am no Greek, hath not th'advantage.
        And of course, no Roman:
        he can take no risk that matters,
175   the risk of beauty least of all.

        But I have my kin, if for no other reason than
        (as he said, next of kin) I commit myself, and,
        given my freedom, I'd be a cad
        if I didn't. Which is most true.

180   It works out this way, despite the disadvantage.
        I offer, in explanation, a quote:
        si j'ai du goût, ce n'est guères
        que pour la terre et les pierres.

        Despite the discrepancy (an ocean   courage   age)
185   this is also true: if I have any taste
        it is only because I have interested myself
        in what was slain in the sun

                I pose you your question:

        shall you uncover honey / where maggots are?

190   I hunt among stones

THE PRAISES

She who was burned more than half her body skipped out of death

Observing
that there are five solid figures, the Master
(or so Aetius reports, in the *Placita*)
5 concluded that
the Sphere of the Universe arose from
the dodecahedron

          whence Alexander,
          appearing in a dream to Antiochus,
10   showed him
          And on the morrow, the enemy (the Galates)
          ran before it,
          before the sign, that is

1
By Filius Bonaci, his series, rediscovered Pisa 1202, we shall attack,
15 for it, too, proceeds asymptotically toward the graphic and tangible, the law
now determined to be
phi
          its capital role in the distribution of
          leaves   seeds   branches on a stem (ex.,
20   the ripe sun-flower)

          the ratios 5/8, 8/13
          in the seed-cones of fir-trees,
          the ratio 21/34
          in normal daisies

25   Pendactylism is general in the animal kingdom.
          But crystals... there, pentagonal forms or lattices
          do not, can not appear

So we have it: star and jelly fish, the sea urchin.
And because there is an ideal and constant angle which,
30 for leaves and branches on a stem, produces
the maximum exposition to light, that light vertical,
fruit blossoms the briar rose the passion flower
But lilies tulips the hyacinth, like crystals...

Here we must stop And ponder For nature,
35 though she is, as you know (so far, that is,
as it is allowed to a mortal to know) from all points of view
similar to herself, yet minerals...

    o, that's not fair, let
    woman keep her jewels, odd man
40   his pleasure of her glow, let
    your lady Nephritite
    pumice her malachite, paint
    her lids green against the light

Sd he:
45   to dream takes no effort
     to think is easy
       to act is more difficult
   but for a man to act after he has taken thought, this!
   is the most difficult thing of all

2
50 We turn now to Ammonius,
who was present when Nero was,
who is full of delights,
& who smiles quickly

   the epiphanies, he says, in this case are four:
55 1st, to such as begin to learn & to inquire,
   the Pythian response,
   with flute

(2) when part of the truth is glimpsed, the sun
(a creature of four-fold eyes and heads,
60   of a ram   a bull   a snake   the bright-eyed lion)
This is little, even though the drum
is added

When a person has got the knowledge, Ammonius
(and he does not mean to be ambiguous)
65   confers one overwhelming title:
he says a man may then call himself OF THEBES. He may sing

The last, and triumphant mode, I leave, as he leaves it,
untranslated: when men are active, enjoy thought, that is to say
when they talk, they are LESKENOI. They rage

70   Which is why what is related must remain enigmatic
And why Ammonius excepts, from these epiphanies,
those who are entirely brutish.

Which brings us to what concerns us in the present inquiry.

Avert, avert, avoid
75   pollution, to be clean
in a dirty time

                         O Wheel, aid us
                         to get the gurry off

You would have a sign. Look:
80   to fly? a fly can do that;
to try the moon? a moth
as well; to walk on water? a straw
precedes you

                         O Wheel! draw
85   that truth
                         to my house

Appendices

```
              Like pa does, not like sis,
              on all detractors, piss, o advertised earth!
              And you, o lady Moon, observe my love,
 90           whence it arose

              Whence it arose,
              and who it is who sits,
              there at the base of the skull, locked
              in his throne of bone, that mere pea of bone
 95           where the axes meet, cross-roads of the system
              god, converter, discloser, he will answer,
              will look out, if you will look, look!

              3
              What has been lost
              is the secret of secrecy, is
100           the value, viz., that the work get done, and quickly,
              without the loss of due and profound respect for
              the materials

              which is not so easy as it sounds, nor
              can it permit the dispersion which follows from
105           too many having too little
              knowledge

                                  Says Iamblichus:
              by shipwreck, he perished (Hippasus, that is)
              the first to publish (write down, divulge)
110           the secret,
              the construction of, from 12 pentagons,
              the sphere

              "Thus was he punished for his impiety"

              What is necessary is
115           containment,
              that that which has been found out by work may, by work, be passed on
              (without due loss of force)
              for use
                    USE

120           "And they took over power, political power, in Gr Greece, including
              Sicily, and maintained themselves, even after the Master died, until,
              at Metapontum, the mob

              "Only Philalaos, and Lysis, did not perish in the fire. Later,
              Archytas it was, pupil of Philalaos, who, friend to Plato, initiated him,
125           and, at Tarentum


              4
              Which is about what we had to say,
              the clues, anyhow

              What belongs to art and reason is
                                        the knowledge of
130                                                   consequences

              L da V, his notebook:

                         Every natural action obeys by
                         the straightest possible process
```

Notes

INTRODUCTION

1. Sherman Paul, *Olson's Push* (Baton Rouge: Louisiana State University Press, 1978), p. xv.
2. Edward Halsey Foster, *Understanding the Black Mountain Poets* (Columbia: University of South Carolina Press, 1995), p. 49.
3. Nina Baym et al., eds., *The Norton Anthology of American Literature*, 3d ed. (New York: W. W. Norton, 1979), p. 2426.
4. Quoted on p. 48 of Olson's *Call Me Ishmael*.
5. See F. O. Matthiessen, *American Renaissance* (New York: Oxford University Press, 1941), p. xviii, where Matthiessen acknowledges Olson's "generosity in letting me make use of what he tracked down in his investigation of Melville's reading." See also footnotes on pp. 209, 413, 415, and 458.
6. Fielding Dawson, "On Olson" *Sagetrieb* 1 (spring 1982): 129.
7. Quoted in Tom Clark's *Charles Olson*, p. 81.
8. Monroe Engel, as an editor with Reynal and Hitchcock, saw *Call Me Ishmael* through the press. Olson's many letters to him are held in Harvard University Library.
9. See letter no. 9 (dated probably 20 October 1948) of the Robert Payne Correspondence in *Minutes of the Charles Olson Society* 14 (April 1996).
10. Letter to Vincent Ferrini dated 6 October 1949 (at Storrs).
11. The anthology was reissued several times as *The New American Poetry* (the dates "1945–1960" being dropped from the title as the decade wore on) until in 1982 Grove Press replaced it with *The Postmoderns: The New American Poetry Revisited*, edited by Donald Allen and George Butterick. The format and selection of the original edition was not replaced in our memories.
12. Guy Davenport, *Every Force Evolves a Form* (San Francisco: North Point Press, 1987), p. 97.
13. Guy Davenport "Scholia and Conjectures for Olson's 'The Kingfishers'" *boundary 2* II, Nos. 1 and 2 (fall 1973–winter 1974): 252.
14. The lecture "The Scholar as Critic" was published in *Shenandoah* and collected in *Every Force Evolves a Form* (pp. 84–98; quotation on p. 97). I do not know anything quite so gracious in the annals of scholarship as this remark of Davenport's. I hope that if Guy finds his explication being confronted at various points he will not think me ungrateful, but just doing what he proposed I should.
15. George Butterick, "Charles Olson's 'The Kingfishers' and the Poetics of Change" *American Poetry* 6 (winter 1989): 28–69. I first saw the piece in Italian,

in *Black Mountain: Poesia e Poetica*, edited by Annalisa Goldoni and Marina Morbiducci (Rome: 1987). For a discussion of Fernand, see chap. 1 (below).

Chapter 1. Anti-Wasteland

1. Letter dated March 1949 by internal evidence, in Special Collections Library, State University of New York at Stony Brook. See letter no. 16 in *Minutes* 14 (April 1996).
2. "GrandPa, GoodBye" in Seelye, p. 105.
3. "With Forced Fingers Rude" *Four Pages* 2 (February 1948): 1.
4. Quoted by Helen Gardner in *The Sources of Four Quartets* (New York: Oxford University Press, 1977), p. 34. Pound had forwarded the postcard to Eliot to get his reaction. Eliot did not return it, so it is still among Eliot's papers.
5. Olson noted in his copy of Eliot's *Collected Poems, 1909–1935* (New York: Harcourt, Brace, 1936) opposite part I of "Burnt Norton": "This is a beautiful passage . . . such a beautiful poem." Quoted by von Hallberg, p. 151.
6. Helen Gardner in *The Sources of Four Quartets* (p. 34) is quoting a typewritten note that Eliot attached to Olson's postcard in his files.
7. Helen Gardner, as previously cited, p. 141.
8. Charles Olson, "Human Universe," in *Selected Writings*, p. 54.
9. *Selected Writings*, p. 56.
10. "I, Maximus of Gloucester, to You" in *The Maximus Poems* (I.6).
11. Robert Creeley, preface to Charles Olson's *Mayan Letters* (Mallorca: Divers Press, 1953), included in Creeley's *A Quick Graph* (San Francisco: Four Seasons Foundation, 1970), p. 159. It should be stressed that "The Kingfishers" was a prelude to Olson's Mexico trip of February–July 1951, not a consequence of it as Carol Kyle assumes in "The Mesoamerican Cultural Past and Charles Olson's *The Kingfishers*," *Alcheringa* 1.2 (1975), pp. 68–71.
12. *Selected Writings*, p. 59.
13. M. L. Rosenthal, *The New Poets* (New York: Oxford University Press, 1967), p. 164.
14. Eric Mottram "A Pig-headed Father and the New Wood," *London Magazine* NS 2.9 (December 1962): 72.
15. Butterick, p. 36. Not knowing of this conversation and the true circumstances before Butterick published his 1989 article, I had always been tempted to take the party to be a dream of Olson's, like "The Librarian" in *Selected Writings*, pp. 217–19. It certainly has a dream-like quality, which can now be explained as due to the weirdness of the actual event.
16. Peter Blanc letter of 7 May 1975, quoted by Butterick, p. 36.
17. Letter of 8 May 1975 in Butterick, p. 37.
18. Letter 30 May 1953 in *Corman Correspondence* II, p. 62.
19. "These Days" in *Collected Poems*, p. 106. It was sent to William Carlos Williams on 12 January 1950, and to Frances Boldereff, Caresse Crosby, Fielding Dawson, and presumably others, around the same time.
20. The page is transcribed in full in chap. 8(I).
21. "Under the Mushroom" *Muthologos* I, p. 59.
22. Butterick (p. 35) quotes more from Osbert Sitwell's book.
23. The letter to Josef Albers of 7 October 1948 is now in the Black Mountain College archive held at the State Archives of North Carolina, Raleigh, N.C.

24. The prose note, the first item in the "Kingfishers" file at Storrs, is quoted in full in chap. 2(II).
25. Sherman Paul *Olson's Push* (previously cited), p. 12.
26. Guy Davenport *Every Force Evolves a Form* (previously cited), p. 95.
27. Seelye, p. 98. Olson heard the phrase during his visit to Pound of 19 March 1946 (Seelye, p. 78).
28. Olson saw parts of the *Pisan Cantos* in typescript and bought the volume on publication. See *Charles Olson's Reading*, p. 65.
29. For example, in "Projective Verse" *Selected Writings*, p. 19, and at Berkeley in 1965, after he had met Pound again at Spoleto (*Muthologos* 1, p. 133).
30. Anonymous review (probably by the editor, Richard Wirtz Emerson) in *Golden Goose* 7 (April 1954): 135.
31. Bibliography of *Mayan Letters* in *Selected Writings*, p. 129.
32. Undated note of about August 1948 at Storrs, published in *OLSON* 5, p. 44.
33. *Selected Writings*, p. 26.
34. Butterick, p. 34. See also *Guide*, p. xxiv.

CHAPTER 2. POLITICS

1. Storrs notebook "Faust-Buch Washington Spring 1947."
2. Clark, p. 90.
3. Charles Olson, "Death in the Afternoon," *Wesleyan Cardinal* 1:3 (February 1933): 92–95.
4. "The K" in *Selected Writings*, p. 159; *Collected Poems*, p. 14.
5. Storrs notebook "1942 Jan.—ca. March 4."
6. "Apollonius of Tyana" in *Selected Writings*, p. 145.
7. Davenport, p. 252.
8. Olson quoted the line in "Projective Verse" to illustrate the point, *Selected Writings*, p. 23.
9. *Dahlberg Correspondence*, p. 51.
10. *Plutarch's Morals: Theosophical Essays*, translated by C. W. King, Bohn's Classical Library (London: George Bell, 1908), p. 174. Olson's flyleaf inscription reads: "many years many times many poems."
11. C. G. Jung and C. Kerenyi, *Essays on a Science of Mythology* (New York: Pantheon, 1949), pp. 69–70. The marginal note is probably of December 1964, but Olson bought the volume on publication and could have been aware in 1949 of the archetypal emphasis that Jung and Kerenyi placed on Delphi.
12. Tape recording in Simon Fraser University Contemporary Literature Collection, 16 August 1963. It was not, in fact, two years before the taking of Peking but only two months.
13. Letter to Ben Shahn of 10 May 1949 (Archives of American Art, New York).
14. Ken Auletta, "A Certain Poetry," *New Yorker* (6 June 1983): 46. See also Ken Auletta, *The Art of Corporate Success: The Story of Schlumberger* (New York: Penguin, 1985), where we find on p. 40: "Olson and his wife, Constance, became special friends of Riboud's. Every two or three months, Riboud took the train to Washington to spend a weekend with them. The three would stay up talking until dawn, sleep until midafternoon, talk until dawn."
15. Olson dedicated to Jean Riboud the short essay entitled "The Resistance" (*Selected Writings*, pp. 13–14). See later discussion in chap. 5(II).
16. Butterick (p. 58) transcribes the undated letter at Storrs.

17. The copy of *The White Pony* in the Olson Archive at Storrs is inscribed by Payne to Ezra Pound. See *Charles Olson's Reading*, p. 72.
18. Posthumously published in *boundary 2* (Olson issue), pp. 1–4, quotation, p. 3. Date about 11 May 1948. A later version, "About Space" (typescript at Storrs) added a further Payne-like comment: "the will of Asia is already dictating the shape of prospective man's society on the earth."
19. Payne was already working on his *Mao Tse-Tung*, published the following year. See *Charles Olson's Reading*, p. 268.
20. "This is Yeats Speaking," *Partisan Review* 13 (winter 1946): 139–142, included in *Human Universe*, pp. 99–102; and in Seelye, along with the drafts, pp. 27–31.
21. *Fiery Hunt*, p. xiv, where Butterick is quoting notes Olson made for a lecture on 29 July 1948.
22. *Boundary 2*, p. 2.

Chapter 3. Modes of Form

1. *Selected Writings*, p. 16. "Projective Verse" was written in draft form on 9 February 1950. After some rewriting it was accepted by *Poetry New York* on 3 April 1950 and published in issue No. 3 (summer 1950).
2. *The Encyclopaedia Britannica*, 11th ed. (New York: Encyclopaedia Britannica, 1910–11), "Kingfisher" entry pp. 808–9.
3. Olson had bought, among the batch of books of September 1948, John Lyly, *Euphues, the Anatomy of Wit & Euphues and His England*, edited by Edward Arber (London: Constable, 1934).
4. *Collected Poems*, p. 78. "Siena," written about 20–30 July 1948, is made up of descriptions of Giovanni di Paolo's paintings, and ends: "we who are awkward ask."
5. "Causal Mythology" (July 1965) in *Muthologos* I, p. 94.
6. One might also note Olson's later slap at the political seductress, Madame Chiang Kai-shek, who, in 1943 and again in 1948, turned up in Washington, D.C., to try to boost her husband's fortunes:

>   . . . that international doll,
> has to have silk, when she is put up
>   (why is she put up with)
> in the white house
>
>   (*Maximus Poems* I.35)

7. Letter to Otto Kahn of 12 September 1927 in *The Letters of Hart Crane 1916–1932* edited by Brom Weber (Berkeley and Los Angeles: University of California Press, 1965), p. 305.
8. *Collected Poems*, p. 4; *A Nation of Nothing But Poetry*, p. 17.
9. Alan C. Golding, *Go Contrary, Go Sing: Charles Olson's Early Poetry and Poetics* (Ph.D. dissertation, University of Chicago 1980), p. 209.
10. See Wilbert Snow "A Teacher's View," *The Massachusetts Review* 12 (winter 1971): 41–42, where we also read that in Professor Alec Cowie's American Literature class, Olson "wrote an essay on George Herbert's influence on the poetry of Ralph Waldo Emerson which was so excellent that Cowie gave it the only A plus Cowie ever gave in his life."
11. Charles Olson, "The Poetry of William Butler Yeats" (Snow Papers, Wesleyan University Library, Special Collections), typescript p. 7.

164 NOTES TO CHAPTER 4

12. "Fifty Years of Intercollegiate Debating at Wesleyan University" (Wesleyan University Library, 1950).
13. Charles J. Olson "An Essay Entitled 'Progress,'" 13 February 1929 (Wesleyan University Library) holograph manuscript.
14. "Speakers Forceful at Poorly Attended Anti-War Meeting Friday," *Clark News* (13 November 1935), reprinted in the Charles Olson issue of *Maps* 4 (1971): 46.
15. Storrs notebook, "1932 Mar. 1–1934 Mar. 25"—entry for 15 December 1932.
16. Sergei M. Eisenstein, *The Film Sense*, translated and edited by Jay Leyda (New York: Harcourt, Brace, 1947), pp. 4, 7–8, 76. A second collection, similarly edited and published, *Film Form* (1949), was, in Butterick's opinion (p. 31), also available to Olson for "The Kingfishers."
17. The text is not at present known. Referring to *Call Me Ishmael*, Olson told Ann Charters in a letter of 14 February 1968 "that something which the book is was immediately reflected in a cable from Serge Eisenstein"—*Olson/Melville*, p. 11.

Chapter 4. Recurrences

1. It is the Modern Library edition (no date of publication given), which contains both *History of the Conquest of Mexico* and *History of the Conquest of Peru* (though clearly Olson read only the former). The volume was deposited by the poet with his sister-in-law Jean Kaiser around 1958. It was purchased by the present writer in 1989. For some unaccountable reason, it was not among the books that George Butterick saw when he visited Jean Kaiser (then Mrs. Radoslovich) and went through the books in her possession. The books he saw were listed, with annotations, in "Olson's Reading: A Preliminary Report," published serially in the first seven issues of *OLSON: Journal of the Charles Olson Archives* (1974–1977). The William Prescott listed there is the Aztec edition published by Tandy, Wheeler and Co. (Denver, 1873 and 1902), of which Olson had in his library only two of the five volumes. These volumes were unmarked. It is now certain that he did not use these old volumes but the Modern Library one-volume edition.
2. Manuscript notes on a Harvard lecture, 15 March 1939 (Storrs). The quotations in this paragraph are from the New Directions 1956 edition of William Carlos Williams's *In the American Grain*.
3. "First Facts," notes of about December 1946, published in *OLSON* 5, p. 25.
4. "Captain John Smith," *Black Mountain Review* 1 (spring 1954), reprinted in *Human Universe*, pp. 131–134, quotation on p. 133.
5. A Library of Congress call-slip indicates Olson asked for *Cabeza de Vaca's Great Journey* (Washington, D.C.: Pan American Union, 1942). For other research into this figure, see *Charles Olson's Reading*, p. 56; p. 254, n. 12.
6. Letter to Constance Olson at Storrs, undated, but probably about 5 March 1941.
7. *OLSON* 5, p. 14. Balboa's discovery of the Pacific is in Prescott, p. 517. In his "Key West II" notebook of 1945, Olson mentions "notes on a poem to be called 'West' you wrote 4 years ago" (*OLSON* 5, p. 11); this reference is now satisfactorily explained as to the "Outline" of 1941.
8. "OPERATION RED, WHITE & BLACK," *OLSON* 5, pp. 27–31, undated but probably January 1947.

9. "Guggenheim Fellowship Proposal, 1948" *OLSON* 5, pp. 32–36, probably written January 1948.

Chapter 5. Self

1. *Plutarch's Morals* (King ed.), pp. 190–92. Ammonius is speaking. The dots are in the original and indicate a missing phrase in the manuscript.
2. Davenport (p. 250) thinks that Olson may have taken this line from Pablo Neruda as well as from Plutarch. He explains (p. 255) that Neruda's line "y no una muerta, sino muchas muertes" in *Macchu Picchu* means that "men with a life as hard as the Peruvians in their isolated mountain fastnesses die difficulty by difficulty." This idea of hardship as serial death is significantly different from Plutarch's stages of life, one dying into the other.
3. *Collected Poems*, pp. 80–81. In the note on p. 648, the date of Dahlberg's letter must now be revised.
4. This sounds like a paraphrase of Plutarch chap. XVIII, but any specific source for the quotation is at present unknown. It is used by Olson again, in a somewhat different mood, in the letter to Natasha Goldowski discussed in section 5(II).
5. This and the following two quotations from the "Human Universe" essay can be found in *Selected Writings*, pp. 54–56.
6. "Projective Verse," *Selected Writings*, p. 24.
7. "The Resistance" may have been put into a final form as a wedding present for Jean Riboud (married 1 October 1949), to whom it was dedicated on publication in *Four Winds* (winter 1953).
8. Martin Duberman in his *Black Mountain* book notes that Natasha Goldowski gave a seminar based on galley proofs she had received of *Cybernetics*: "A lot of people sat in, including Olson" (p. 374).
9. Mary Emma Harris, *The Arts at Black Mountain College*, p. 110. Natasha Goldowski wrote a piece on "High Speed Computing Machines" for issue no. 1 of the first series of the *Black Mountain Review* (June 1951).
10. "Proprioception" in *Additional Prose*, p. 17. An alternative definition given there is: "the 'body' of us as object which spontaneously or of its own order produces experience of, 'depth.'"
11. *Selected Writings*, pp. 50–51. Olson's source for Riemann's use of "discrete" and "continuous" is Herman Weyl's *Philosophy of Mathematics and Natural Science* (Princeton: Princeton University Press, 1949), p. 43.

Chapter 6. Pejorocracy

1. This quotation from Prof. Merk's lecture is found in notes made by Joseph C. Borden, who took the course in the fall of 1930. See the facsimile reproduction of his notes in *Merk and Olson*, edited by Ralph Maud, a pamphlet produced for use at Simon Fraser University in 1970—the quotation is on p. 8.
2. The dance-play "The Fiery Hunt" was published posthumously in *The Fiery Hunt and Other Plays*, pp. 23–24.
3. Merton Sealts, *Pursuing Melville* (Madison: University of Wisconsin Press, 1982), p. 94.
4. Olson owned at that time the three-volume Temple Classics *Divine Com-*

edy published by Dent. The reference to "the yellow of the eternal rose" appears on p. 371 of the Paradiso volume (London: J. M. Dent, n.d.).

5. Postcard to Monroe Engel of 11 May 1948 (at Harvard): "Actually, I need more than it contains. What I was after was DE VULGARE ELOQUENTIA." Olson found a larger selection from that work of Dante's in a book he already had, *The Great Critics*, rev. ed., edited by Smith and Parks (New York: Norton, 1939), pp. 147–48.

6. "The Long Poem" *OLSON* 5, p. 38.

7. The Temple Classics *Paradiso*, canto xxx, p. 369.

8. "The Praises" (lines 87–88) has:

> Like pa does, not like sis,
> on all detractors, piss, o advertised earth!

A letter to Frances Boldereff of 10 January 1950 offers something of a gloss. (The object of Olson's annoyance here is an unnamed book.)

> It outrages that thing I cannot put another word on, than pudor. I call it mysterious. For it is, that resistance in us to good when it is exposed before us without its proper cloak, the cloak which returns it to us as object, for use.

9. *Creeley Correspondence* 3, p. 131. Olson repeated the point in a letter from Mexico 20 March 1951 (*Selected Writings*, p. 93): "like I tried to say, abt *leaving* the difficulties, not removing them, by *buying* the improvements so readily available at the corner. You buy something all right, but what gets forgotten is, that you sell, in that moment of buying—you sell a whole disposition of self which very soon plunders you just where you are not looking."

10. Olson read David Rousset's novel *L'univers concentrationaire* (Paris: 1946), being given it, presumably by Jean Riboud, on publication. Rousset was also a survivor of Buchenwald.

11. Shakespeare's *Timon of Athens* IV.1.17: "Domestic awe, night-rest, and neighbourhood." Olson had quoted Timon's "I am sick of this false world" speech as the epigraph to chap. 3 of his master's thesis on Melville (Wesleyan University, 1933). In his discussion of Timon's speech, Davenport expresses indebtedness to Gerrit Lansing "for pointing out this quotation" (p. 258). I am happy to repeat this acknowledgment.

Chapter 7. The Advantage

1. Olson came to think the Quetzalcoatl material "was sufficient unto itself" (*Selected Writings*, p. 75). It apparently became a separate poem entitled "Not the Fall of a Sparrow." It was read by Olson as background for a dance in "Exercises in Theatre" at BMC 29 August 1949, but a copy is not at the moment known. Appendix F shows Olson beginning to write about Quetzalcoatl from his source, *The Maya and their Neighbors* (London: D. Appleton-Century Co., 1940), pp. 165–66.

2. "Put him this way. . . ." *Collected Poems*, pp. 70–71, dated in the notes as from "about 1948–1950."

3. Wallace Fowlie, *Rimbaud* (New York: New Directions, 1946), p. 42.

4. *Additional Prose*, p. 4; *Human Universe*, p. 114; in a letter to Frances Boldereff 28 March 1950; and undoubtedly elsewhere.

5. "The Present Is Prologue," *Additional Prose*, p. 40, written November 1952.

6. *Additional Prose*, p. 40. George Butterick in "Charles Olson and the Postmodern Advance," *The Iowa Review* 11 (fall 1980): 4–27, traces Olson's use of the term *postmodern*, beginning with its occurrence in a letter to Robert Creeley of August 1951 (*Creeley Correspondence* 7, p. 75).

7. Olson's notes on his 9 February 1948 visit to Pound at St. Elizabeths (Seelye, p. 93).

8. Undated letter to Pound (Indiana University), probably of 9 February 1948.

9. This and the next quotation are in "GrandPa, GoodBye" (Seelye, p. 101).

10. The "I" of "I commit myself" etc. should be seen as Pound's speaking of himself. This is clearer in a draft in the "Kingfishers" file:

> But I have my kin, if for no other reason than
> as he said (next of kin), I commit myself,
> and, given my freedom, he said,
> I'd be a cad if I didn't.
> Which is most true.

Clarity suffers in Olson's rewriting of these lines, changing the parentheses and deleting the second "he said." We should ignore the slight ambiguity that the revision has injected into the lines and take it that the sense has not changed. See also the worksheet, Appendix F.

11. Letter to Dorothy Pound (Indiana University). Olson went on to express concern over Pound's health.

12. A typescript of the finished poem as we have it, sent to Michael Lekakis, is dated "black mt / july 20 xlix."

13. Olson makes this remark in *Special View of History*, p. 31.

14. The "who" is typed over with a "he" in the letter to Caresse Crosby, and "he" appears in all the worksheets.

15. The words "hath not th'advantage" compel us to think of Shakespeare or his contemporaries, but the concordance indicates that no such phrase exists in Shakespeare, and no one has discovered it anywhere else.

Chapter 8. "The Praises"

1. The first part of this outline was discussed to some extent in chap. 4(I).

2. The poet took this line out of a letter he had written to Robert Payne on 24 February 1949, thus giving us an approximate date for the worksheet.

3. The following phrases from Plutarch (p. 189) are used: "Good is imagined as being manifested five kinds. . . . 'In the sixth period still the rage of song'. . . . 'On the sixth day of the new moon, when you conduct the Pythia to the Townhall, the first casting of the three lots takes place. . . . You throw neither three nor two—is it not so?' 'It is so,' replied Nicander; 'but the reason must not be divulged to others.' . . . So the list of the arithmetical and mathematical praises of the letter E . . . is now concluded."

4. In some later notes (dated 15 December 1959 at Storrs) Olson quotes this line and adds the query, "Mrs Shorey?" This seems to indicate that the reference is to an actual person. I see no point in going so far afield as to speculate, as Maxine Apsel does in her article "'The Praises'" in *boundary 2*, that we have

168   NOTES TO CHAPTER 8

here "possibly a reference to the corpse of Hypatia, a learned professor whose death marked the decay of Alexandrian mathematics" (p. 265).

5. Maxine Apsel in *boundary 2* does not appear to be aware of Ghyka as a source for "The Praises," whereas Robert von Hallberg specifies some pages of Ghyka in his extensive discussion of the poem. For the sake of completeness, we can list the lines of the poem (i.e., most of parts 1 and 3) that have their source in Ghyka:

"The Praises" (lines)	Ghyka (pp.)
2–13	114
14–24	13–14
25–33	18–19, 14
34–37	115
107–113	113
120–125	116
131–133	173

6. For instance, *Creeley Correspondence* 7, p. 239; and p. 273, n. 163. The exact source in Novalis for the particular wording has not been found.

7. The lines appeared in the version in *New Directions* XII (1950) and in *In Cold Hell, In Thicket* (1953) but were dropped without any other changes in the poem for the reprinting in *The Distances* (1960).

8. At the time of the reprinting of the poem in *Selected Writings*, James Laughlin wrote to Olson asking him if he did not mean "undue" rather than "due" here. Olson replied in a postcard of 20 August 1969: "'due' is OK." The sense must be, then, that the work needs to be passed on without *any* loss of force, not even a loss that might be normally expected.

9. "The Grandfather-Father Poem" (October 1964) in *Collected Poems*, p. 617. The same picture of his grandfather occurs in "An Ode on Nativity" *Collected Poems*, p. 246.

10. Quoted in Butterick's introduction (p. vii) to *The Post Office*.

11. The typescript dated 5 June 1947 was later sent to Henry Murray with a letter of 31 March 1949 (i.e., during work on "The Kingfishers"). With some changes, it was published as "Move Over" (*Collected Poems*, pp. 66–67).

12. This quotation from Babson (p. 165) is included in notes entitled "WEST" printed in *OLSON* 5, p. 41 (date possibly May 1948).

13. Olson is quoting his source, G. R. S. Mead *Apollonius of Tyana* (1901), in "Apollonius of Tyana" *Selected Writings*, p. 155.

14. Duberman, pp. 286 and 317.

15. Letter to Jonathan Williams of 26 April 1961 (Buffalo). Fuller's *Untitled Epic Poem on the History of Industrialization* was published as Jargon 44 (Highlands, N.C.: Nantahala Foundation, 1962).

16. Ghyka, p. 113: "Hippasus who was a Pythagorean but, owing to his being the first to publish and write down the construction of the sphere from 12 pentagons (the construction of the dodecahedron), perished by shipwreck for his impiety." And on p. 114: "Pythagoras, seeing that there are 5 solid figures . . . said that the Sphere of the Universe arose from the dodecahedron." From which, lines 2–7 of "The Praises":

> Observing
> that there are five solid figures, the Master

> (or so Aetius reports, in the Placita)
> concluded that
> the Sphere of the Universe arose from
> the dodecahedron.

17. Buckminster Fuller had published his *Nine Chains to the Moon* in 1938.

Chapter 9. "The Kingfishers": Epilogue

1. Article by Burton Hatlen in *Contemporary Literature* 30 (1989): 546–572; quotation on p. 571.
2. Letter to Ben Shahn in the Archives of American Art, New York.
3. Clark, p. 87.
4. Frances K. Pohl, *Ben Shahn: New Deal Artist in a Cold War Climate, 1947–1954* (Austin: University of Texas Press, 1989), pp. 1–2.
5. *Creeley Correspondence* 9, pp. 69–72, and p. 292, n. 62: "A Search of Olson's FBI file reveals it was his contact with Polish and eastern European groups at the close of World War II that prompted the Bureau's interest." Though this visit by FBI agents on 1 February 1952 had, thus, nothing to do with the publication of "The Kingfishers," Olson in writing to Creeley (p. 72) was thinking back to the poem: "I dealt with these two men not as agents but as two new-met men—and how otherwise? how be canny without being theirs? how stay free except on exactly the act of freedom? And the communication one? 'I'd be a cad, if I didn't,' eh?" In other words, Olson decided to commit himself to freedom by behaving freely.
6. In a letter to Frances Boldereff of 23 March 1950 (Storrs).
7. It is not at the moment confirmed whether or not "The Kingfishers" appeared in Italy before the translation by Giulio Saponaro in *Poesia Degli Ultimi Americani*, edited by Fernando Pivano (Milan: Feltrinelli Editore, 1964).
8. Ray West had published "There Was a Youth Whose Name Was Thomas Granger" in *Western Review* 11 (spring 1947), and "Siena" in *Western Review* 13 (winter 1949).
9. Even Payne had balked a little. He wrote to Olson on 5 February 1950, suggesting that the Italian lines (152–53) be cut because Pound had done too much quoting of Italian. The lines stayed, but a bibliographical reference (see Appendix C) was dropped.
10. *Maximus Poems*, "Letter 2" (I.5). This is something Olson got in an early talk with Edward Dahlberg: "one of the finest pieces of wisdom i acquired from you is, people do not change" (*Dahlberg Correspondence*, p. 108). It is not entirely clear whether Olson thought of it in relation to the poem's "will to change," or it remained a bit of Dahlberg wisdom.
11. *OLSON* 10, p. 68. The quotation that ends this paragraph is from the same page.
12. Quotation from the soundtrack of the NET film of Olson in Gloucester (*Muthologos* 1, p. 186). For further comment on this point, see Robin Blaser, "The Violets: A Cosmological Reading of a Cosmology," *Process Studies* 13 (spring 1983): 8–37, revised as "The Violets: Charles Olson and Alfred North Whitehead," *Line* 2 (fall 1983): 61–103.
13. Henry Corbin, *Avicenna and the Visionary Recital*, translated by Willard Trask (New York: Pantheon Books, 1960), p. 148.
14. "On Black Mountain (II)," an interview in Gloucester with Andrew S. Leinoff (April 1969), *OLSON* 8, p. 79.

Index

Acheson, Dean, 42
Aeneas, 102
Africa, 96
Ahab, 14, 87, 89
Aiken, Conrad, 101
Alabama, 127
Albers, Josef, 25, 28, 29, 161
Alcheringa, 161
Alexander, 114
Allen, Donald, 17, 127, 128, 160
Altamira, 79
America/American, 30, 36, 42, 45, 49, 55, 56, 65, 66, 69, 70, 71, 72, 85, 86, 98, 100, 105, 106, 118, 123, 124
American Poetry, 19, 30, 36, 37, 132, 160
Amherst, 56
Ammonius, 108, 165
Angkor Vat, 25, 28, 29, 45, 46, 48, 62
Anthology (Greek), 38
Antiochus, 114
Apollo, 38
Apollonius of Tyana, 35, 70, 115, 168
Appleseed, Johnny, 91
Apsel, Maxine, 167, 168
archeopteryx, 55
Archives of American Art, 19, 162, 169
Aristotle, 78, 104
Asia, 41, 85, 163
Athenaeus, 38
Atlantic, 65, 66, 70
Auletta, Ken, 162
Avicenna, 130, 167
Aztec, 62, 64, 67, 68, 85, 97

Babson, John J., 114, 168
Bagatto, Senor, 14, 120
Balboa, Vasco Núñez de, 71, 164
Baym, Nina, 160
Bérard, Victor, 16, 104
Berkeley, 52, 66, 162
Bible, 98

Black Mountain College, 13, 16, 17, 28, 49, 79, 81, 105, 115, 116, 125, 129, 131, 161, 166, 167, 169
Black Mountain: Poesia e Poetica, 161
Black Mountain Review, 164, 165
Blanc, Peter and Joan, 25, 26, 28, 38, 161
Blaser, Robin, 19, 88, 169
Boer, Charles, 19
Boldereff, Frances, 31, 35, 59, 60, 70, 88, 100, 106, 118, 123, 128, 161, 166, 169
Bollingen, 101, 102
Bonacci, Filius, 110
Borden, Joseph C., 165
Boston, 91
boundary 2, 18, 30, 88, 105, 160, 163, 167, 168
Bowering, George, 19
British, 66
Brooklyn, 54
Brooks, Van Wyck, 75
Browning, Robert, 106
Buchenwald, 40, 79, 80, 90, 166
Buffalo, 19, 105, 128, 168
Butterick, George F., 13, 19, 25, 26, 28, 30, 32, 36, 37, 39, 41, 69, 114, 132, 160, 161, 162, 163, 164, 167, 168
B.V.M. (Blessed Virgin Mary), 22

Cabeza de Vaca, A. N., 69, 70, 71, 72, 102, 109, 164
Cagli, Corrado, 14, 79, 120, 121, 122, 126
Cambodia, 28
cannibalism, 68, 89, 90, 123
Canton, 28
Cantos, 30, 50, 51
Cape Ann, 22
Catullus, 38
Celtic, 56
Chapman, John, 91

170

Index

Charles Olson's Reading, 162, 163, 164
Charters, Ann, 164
Chase, Owen, 89
Chaucer, Geoffrey, 42
Chiang Kai Check, General and Madame, 53, 163
Chicago, 34, 79, 117
China/Chinese, 28, 39, 41, 45, 48, 50, 68, 123
Christian, 85, 114
Chungking, 41
CIO-Political Action Committee, 125
Clare, Saint, 52, 53
Clark, Tom, 33, 160, 162, 169
Clarke, John, 19
Clark News, 164
Clark University, 57
Columbus, Christopher, 54, 71
communism/communist, 39, 40, 41, 118, 125
Confucian, 112
Contemporary Literature, 169
Corbin, Henry, 130, 169
Corman, Cid, 128
Cortez, Hernando, 54, 61, 63, 64, 66, 67, 68, 70, 72
Cowie, Alec, 163
Crane, Hart, 51, 54, 55, 163
Cranston, Alan, 33
Creeley, Robert, 13, 23, 29, 30, 50, 54, 55, 60, 67, 92, 98, 99, 116, 122, 129, 161, 167, 169
Crosby, Caresse, 26, 53, 69, 95, 103, 161, 167
Cummings, E. E., 59
cybernetics, 73, 80, 81, 82, 110, 165
Cyclops, 89

Dahlberg, Edward, 38, 58, 75, 76, 126, 165, 169
Dante, 88, 89, 93, 94, 166
Darwin, Charles, 43
Davenport, Guy, 18, 30, 37, 51, 65, 82, 88, 99, 160, 162, 165, 166
Davis, Elmer, 33
Dawson, Fielding, 16, 160, 161
Delphi/Delphic, 35, 36, 39, 51, 73, 84, 94, 109, 118, 129, 162
Democratic Party, 34, 52, 125
Diaz Del Castillo, Bernal, 68
Domitian, 115
Donner party, 89

Doria, Charles, 105
Dostoevsky, Fyodor, 98
"Drawings in the 4th Dimension" (Cagli), 120, 122
Dry Salvages, 22, 23
Duberman, Martin, 115, 165, 168

E, 35, 38, 39, 45, 63, 64, 73, 84, 108, 109, 110, 118, 119, 129, 167
East/eastern, 39, 45, 67, 85, 86, 105, 123
Edizione D'Argo, 126
Egyptian, 119
Einstein, Albert, 43
Eisenstein, Sergei, 58, 59, 164
Eliot, T. S., 21, 22, 23, 24, 25, 29, 30, 31, 32, 69, 101, 106, 107, 161
Elizabethan, 31, 38, 106
Emerson, Ralph Waldo, 14, 75, 91, 113, 124, 163
Emerson, Richard Wirtz, 162
Encyclopaedia Britannica, 46, 47, 49, 163
Engel, Monroe, 16, 17, 71, 126, 160, 166
English, 40, 66
Eshleman, Clayton, 19
Essays on a Science of Mythology, 39, 162
Euclid, 121
Europe/European, 24, 30, 56, 57, 69, 79, 86, 97

FAO, 91
fascism, 30, 40, 99
Faust, 71
FBI, 125, 169
feedback, 64, 73, 81, 82
Fenollosa, Ernest, 50, 51
Fernand, 17, 18, 19, 25, 26, 28, 29, 45, 63, 108, 161
Ferrini, Vincent, 126, 160
"Fifty Years of Intercollegiate Debating at Wesleyan," 164
Florentine, 52
Foster, Edward Halsey, 13, 160
Fourier, François, 43
Four Pages, 21, 161
Four Winds, 165
Fowlie, Wallace, 97, 166
France/French, 39, 40, 95
Franco, Francisco, 40

Frazer, James G., 43
Freud, Sigmund, 43, 89
Frobenius, Leo, 43, 77
Frost, Robert, 127
Fuller, R. Buckminster, 115, 116, 117, 120, 121, 168, 169
Fyffe, Richard, 20

Gagarin, Yuri, 42
Galates, 114
Gardner, Helen, 22, 161
Gawain, Sir, 114
Gemisto, 31
Gerhardt, Rainer, 98, 124
Gernand, John, 25, 26, 27, 28
Ghyka, Matila, 110, 111, 114, 120, 168
Ginsberg, Allen, 13
Giovanni di Paolo, 52, 53, 163
Gloucester, 14, 22, 23, 105, 114, 169
Golden Goose, 162
Golding, Alan C., 55, 163
Goldoni, Annalisa, 161
Goldowski, Natasha, 79, 81, 165
Greece/Greek, 23, 24, 37, 95, 102, 103, 104, 105, 106, 116, 119, 123
Grove Press, 17, 160
Guggenheim Foundation, 14, 71
Guide to the Maximus Poems, 66, 114, 115, 123, 162

Halcyon, 47
Hall, Donald, 127
Hamlet, 103
Harris, Mary Emma, 81, 116, 117, 165
Harrison, Jane, 119, 128
Harvard University, 14, 21, 63, 86, 160, 164, 166
Hatlen, Burton, 169
Hawthorne, Nathaniel, 70
Hellenism, 105
Hemingway, Ernest and Pauline, 34
Heraclitus, 36, 37, 64, 73, 74, 108, 129
Herbert, George, 75, 163
Herodotus, 38
Hesiod, 38
Hillman, James, 77
Hillyer, Robert, 101
Hindoo, 85
Hines, Jack (grandfather), 113
Hippasus, 117, 168
Hiroshima, 121
Hitler, Adolf, 121

Hittites, 105
Hollywood, 41
Homer/Homeric, 16, 94, 105, 110
Houseman, John, 33
Hudson Review, 126

I Ching, 129
ideogram, 50, 51, 86
Iliad, 104
India, 128
Indiana University, 19, 167
Indians, 69, 86
Indo-Chinese, 62
Institute of Contemporary Arts, 59
Institute of the New Sciences of Man, 129
intent., 19
In the American Grain, 63, 70, 164
Iowa Review, 167
Irish antecedents, 113
Ismaili, 129
Italian language, 68, 169

Jaeger, Werner, 104
Jamestown, 65
Japan/Japanese, 68
Jung, C. G., 162

Kahn, Otto, 163
Kaiser, Jean, 164
Kennan, George, 118
Kenner, Hugh, 50
Kerenyi, C., 39
Keyishian, Harry, 20
Key West, 33, 34, 35, 96, 164
Kierkegaard, Søren, 43
"Know thyself," 36, 38, 40, 82, 94, 95, 96, 109, 129
Kyle, Carol, 161

Lady of Good Voyage, 22, 23
Lafayette College, 56
Lansing, Gerrit, 166
La Salle, René, 71
Lattimore, Owen, 41, 123
Laughlin, James, 20, 127, 168
Lawrence, D. H., 24, 72, 98
Leary, Timothy, 129
Leinoff, Andrew S., 169
Leite, George, 100
Lekakis, Michael, 167

Index 173

Leonardo da Vinci, 111, 120
Leviathan, 119
Levy, Rev. W. T., 22, 23
Lexington, 18
Leyda, Jay, 58, 59, 164
Library of Congress, 32, 33, 164
Line, 169
Lithuanian, 124
Long March, 31, 32, 123
Lowell, Robert, 101
l'univers concentrationaire, 41, 92, 166
Lyly, John, 38, 163
Lyons, 40

MacLeish, Archibald, 33
Madison Square Garden, 34
Malanga, Gerard, 103, 104
Mao Tse-Tung, 32, 38, 39, 40, 41, 45, 48, 51, 63, 86, 92, 108, 163
Maps, 164
Marseilles, 22
Marx, Karl, 43
Marxist/Marxism, 30, 36
Massachusetts Review, 163
Matthiessen, F. O., 14, 160
Maud, Ralph, 18, 165
Maya, 99
Maya and Their Neighbors, 166
McClure, Michael, 13
Mead, G. R. S., 168
Mediterranean, 99
Melville, Herman, 14, 16, 30, 49, 58, 87, 89, 98, 119, 160, 165, 166
Merk, Frederick, 86, 165
Merleau-Ponty, Maurice, 27
Metcalf, Eleanor Melville, 39
Mexico/Mexican, 85, 92, 161, 166
Michelangelo, 24
Middletown, 57
Milton, John, 21, 22
Minutes of the Charles Olson Society, 15, 160, 161
Moby-Dick, 14, 58, 87, 89, 119
Mongolian, 86
Montevallo Review, 126
Montezuma, 61, 62, 63, 64, 66, 71
Moore, Frank, 15, 16, 89
Morbiducci, Marina, 161
Mottram, Eric, 24, 161
Murray, Henry A., 43, 52, 126, 168
Mussolini, Benito, 99

Nazis, 79
Nehru, Jawaharlal, 41
Neruda, Pablo, 30, 36, 165
NET, 169
New American Poetry, 17, 127, 160
New Criticism, 127
New Deal, 125
New Directions, 127, 168
New England, 113, 114
New Jersey, 125
New York City, 15, 116
New Yorker, 40, 162
Noah, 46
Nobel prize, 21
Norman, Dorothy, 14
North Carolina, 17
Norton Anthology of American Literature, 160
Novalis, 111, 168

Oberlin College, 56
object/objectism/objectivist, 27, 31, 49, 95, 122, 127
Odyssey, 16, 89, 104
Office of War Information, 15, 33, 124
OLSON, 69, 71, 94, 102, 105, 162, 164, 165, 166, 168, 169
Olson, Charles: "About Space," 163; *Additional Prose*, 49, 165, 166, 167; "Apollonius of Tyana," 35, 162, 168; "A Bibliography on America for Ed Dorn," 49; "Birth's Obituary," 55; *Call Me Ishmael*, 14, 49, 58, 59, 70, 71, 89, 124, 160, 164; "Captain John Smith," 164; "Causal Mythology," 163; *Collected Poems*, 13, 77, 118, 161, 163, 165, 166, 168; "Conqueror," 77, 80; *Corman Correspondence*, 128, 161; "CREDO," 95; *Creeley Correspondence*, 15, 16, 23, 31, 50, 51, 55, 59, 98, 99, 116, 123, 129, 166, 167, 168, 169; *Dahlberg Correspondence*, 76, 126, 162, 169; "Death in the Afternoon," 162; *The Distances*, 168; "Elegy," 114; "Equal, That Is, to the Real Itself," 82; "An Essay Entitled 'Progress'," 56, 164; "Exercises in Theatre," 166; "The Fiery Hunt"/*The Fiery Hunt*, 87, 163, 165; "First Facts," 164; "For Sappho, Back," 118; "The Grandfather-Father Poem," 168; "GrandPa,

GoodBye," 100, 161, 167; "The Growth of Herman Melville, Prose Writer and Poetic Thinker," 49, 55, 58, 166; "Guggenheim Fellowship Proposal, 1948," 165; "Human Universe"/*Human Universe*, 23, 24, 78, 80, 82, 97, 161, 163, 164, 165, 166; "Ilias," 104; "I, Maximum of Gloucester, to You," 161; *In Cold Hell, In Thicket*, 168; "The K," 35, 37, 162; "La Préface," 79, 80, 120; "Lear and Moby-Dick," 14; "Letter 2," 169; "Letter 7," 114; "The Librarian," 161; "The Long Poem" 102, 166; *The Maximus Poems*, 13, 15, 23, 27, 66, 88, 90, 91, 103, 114, 129, 130, 161, 163, 169; "Maximum to Gloucester, Letter 27 (withheld)," 105; "Maximus, to himself," 103, 104; *Mayan Letters*, 92, 161, 162; "More Notes Toward the Proposition: Man is Prospective," 88; "Move Over," 168; *Muthologos*, 52, 58, 66, 86, 99, 104, 161, 162, 163, 169; "mythography and geometry," 112; *A Nation of Nothing But Poetry*, 163; "Notes for the Proposition: Man is Prospective," 41, 42, 43; "Not the Fall of a Sparrow," 166; "An Ode on Nativity," 168; "On Black Mountain (II)," 169; "Operation Red, White & Black," 164; "An Outline of the Shape and the Characters of a Projected Poem called WEST," 71, 164; "*Paris Review* Interview," 103, 104; "The Poetry of William Butler Yeats," 163; "The Post Office"/*The Post Office*, 113, 114, 168; "The Praises," 13, 57, 93, 108, 109, 110, 111, 112, 113, 114, 116, 117, 118, 120, 121, 126, 127, 132, 166, 167, 168; "The Present is Prologue," 167; "Projective Verse," 13, 31, 44, 45, 48, 49, 51, 59, 60, 67, 88, 106, 117, 127, 128, 162, 163, 165; "Proprioception," 82, 165; "Proteid," 82, 94; "Proteus," 108, 110, 125, 132; "Put him this way. . .," 166; *Red, White, and Black*, 71; "The Resistance," 80, 111, 162, 165; *Selected Writings*, 44, 45, 48, 49, 51, 59, 67, 78, 79, 80, 92, 105, 11, 117, 122, 127, 161, 162, 163, 165, 166, 168; "Siena," 52, 163, 169; "The Songs of Maximus," 90, 91, 92; *Spanish Speaking Americans and the War*, 124; *Special View of History*, 130, 167; "Tanto e Amara," 76, 77, 80; "There Was a Youth Whose Name Was Thomas Granger," 169; "These Days," 27, 118, 161; "This Is Yeats Speaking," 42, 163; *Troilus*, 42; "The True Life of Arthur Rimbaud," 96; "Tutorial: the Greeks," 105; "Under the Mushroom," 161; "WEST," 168; *Y & X*, 121; "You, Hart Crane," 55

Olson, Charles Joseph (CO's father), 76, 113, 114, 115
Olson, Constance (Connie, Contanza), 14, 15, 34, 38, 71, 162, 164
Olson, Mary T. (CO's mother), 76
Olson/Melville, 164
Orphic, 119
Ovid, 47

Pacific, 70, 164
Paris, 98
Partisan Review, 163
Paul, Sherman, 13, 160, 162
Payne, Robert, 17, 21, 22, 23, 41, 42, 43, 126, 160, 163, 167, 169
pejorocracy, 85, 90, 93
Peking, 39, 162
Pepper, Claude, 125
Percy, Thomas, 38
Perse, St.-John, 21
Peru/Peruvians, 86, 165
phenomenology/phenomenologist, 27, 63, 95
Phi Beta Kappa, 113
Philadelphia, 52, 53, 125
Picasso, Pablo, 52
Pisan Cantos, 30, 88, 90, 99, 101, 162
Pivano, Fernanda, 169
Planck, Max, 84
Plato/Platonic, 74, 78, 116
Plutarch, 38, 73, 74, 75, 77, 78, 80, 81, 82, 109, 117, 120, 129, 130, 162, 165, 167
Pocahontas, 54, 65
Poetry, 102
Poetry London, 126
Poetry New York, 127, 163
Pohl, Frances K., 169

polis, 42, 106
Polish groups, 169
Polo, Marco, 68, 89
Pope, Alexander, 56
postmodern, 13, 24, 56, 97, 98, 104, 105, 112, 116, 121, 122, 129, 130, 167
Postmoderns: The New American Poetry Revised, 160
Pound, Dorothy, 21, 101, 167
Pound, Ezra, 13, 22, 30, 31, 37, 42, 50, 51, 52, 55, 59, 88, 90, 94, 99, 100, 101, 102, 161, 162, 163, 167, 169
Powhatan, 65, 66
Prescott, William H., 36, 55, 61, 62, 63, 64, 65, 67, 68, 70, 71, 85, 86, 164
Princeton University, 56
Process Studies, 169
proprioceptive, 82
Proteus/Protean, 110, 125
Prufrock, J. Alfred, 25, 103
Prynne, Jeremy, 13
Pythagoras/Pythagorean, 70, 108, 110, 111, 119, 121, 168

Quetzalcoatl, 71, 94, 109, 166

Radoslovich, Jean, 164
Raleigh, N.C., 161
Renaissance, 43, 52, 66
Renan, Ernest, 43
Reynal and Hitchcock, 160
Riboud, Jean, 39, 40, 162, 165, 166
Riemann, G. F. B., 82, 165
Rimbaud, Arthur, 95, 96, 97, 98, 102, 103, 166
Roman Catholic, 40, 88
Romantic, 23, 103
Rome/Roman, 21, 23, 95, 102, 103, 104, 123
Roosevelt, Franklin D., 15, 34
Rosenstock-Huessy, Eugen, 100
Rosenthal, M. L., 24, 123, 161
Rousset, David, 166
Royal Society, 23
ruins, 29, 30

Sagetrieb, 160
Samson, 98
Sandburg, Carl, 127
Saponaro, Guilio, 169
Saragossa, 100

Saturday Review, 101
Schimmelpfeng, Richard, 20
Schlumberger Corporation, 40, 162
Scientific American, 81, 82
Sealts, Merton M., 87, 165
self, 36, 70, 72, 73, 166
Seelye, Catherine, 22, 100, 161, 162, 163, 167
Shahn, Ben, 39, 124, 125, 162, 169
Shakespeare, William, 14, 66, 67, 92, 94, 166, 167
Shapiro, Karl, 102
Shelley, Percy B., 30
Shenandoah, 160
Sherwood, Robert, 33
Shjarir, 41
Shorey, Mrs., 167
Sienese painting, 52
Simon, John, 128
Simon Fraser University, 18, 162, 165
Sinatra, Frank, 34
Sitter, Willem de, 43
Sitwell, Osbert, 28, 161
Smith, Captain John, 65, 66, 67
Smith, James Harry, 166
Snow, Wilbert, 56, 163
Socrates/Socratic, 38, 129
Sorel, Georges, 43
Southern Illinois University, 19, 26, 95
Southey, Robert, 65
Soviet, 42, 56
Spain/Spaniard/Spanish, 64, 66, 71, 97
"Speakers Forceful at Poorly Attended Anti-War Meeting Friday," 164
Spengler, Oswald, 43
Spoleto, 162
Stanford University, 19, 60
Starbuck, 14
Starkie, Enid, 96
St. Elizabeths Hospital, 22, 30, 167
St. Matthews Cathedral, 25, 29
Stephens, William, 114
Stony Brook (SUNY), 19, 161
Storrs, 14, 19, 20, 27, 29, 31, 33, 35, 39, 43, 53, 57, 63, 76, 79, 80, 82, 94, 95, 96, 104, 108, 112, 113, 118, 120, 121, 126, 132, 160, 162, 163, 164, 167
Sumer, 99, 122

Tarot, 14, 121
Tate, Allen, 101
Theocritus, 38

Thesen, Sharon, 19
Thurn, Ibby von, 16
Tiger's Eye, 30
Timon of Athens, 92, 166
Tlascalan, 65
Troy/Trojan, 104, 115
Truman, Harry S., 34
Twice A Year, 14

Ulysses, 71
United Nations, 91
United States, 39, 40, 124
University of California, 13

Vancouver, 39, 45, 125, 129
Vassar College, 56
Viking Publishers, 71, 88
Von Hallberg, Robert, 118, 124, 161, 168

Wallace, Henry, 34, 125
Washington and Lee University, 18
Washington, D.C., 15, 17, 21, 25, 29, 34, 37, 39, 40, 52, 59, 120, 123, 124, 126, 162, 163
Watts, Charles, 19
Weber, Brom, 163

Webster's Collegiate Dictionary, 82
Wesleyan Cardinal, 162
Wesleyan University, 14, 19, 56, 163, 164, 166
West, Ray B., 126, 169
West/Western, 23, 24, 29, 30, 31, 45, 48, 69, 71, 72, 85, 86, 87, 94, 99, 123
Western Review, 126, 169
Weyl, Hermann, 165
Whitehead, Alfred North, 130, 169
Whitman, Walt, 94
Wiener, Norbert, 73, 81, 110
Wilbur, Richard, 127
Wilcock, Constance, 15
Williams, Jonathan, 116, 168
Williams, William Carlos, 13, 21, 54, 55, 59, 63, 100, 161, 164
Williams College, 56
Worcester, 57

Yale University, 21, 56
Yankee, 91
Yeats, W. B., 42, 56
Yenan, 41
Yucatan, 13, 28, 79, 122, 124

Zeus, 128